When we speak about God in this book, we are referring to God the Father, the Creator of Heaven and Earth, Jesus' Father, "Abba", as he called him.

When we speak about Jesus, we are referring to Jesus Christ, the son of God who became man.

When we speak about the Holy Spirit, we are referring to the Spirit whom Jesus sent to us as our Helper, who assists us at all times.

All scriptures literally quoted from the Old and New Testament, if not otherwise noted, are taken from the New International Version.

Hildegard und Heinrich Becker

About Our Father

About Abba and His children

Bibliographic Information from the German National Library
The German National Library registered this Publication

in the German National Bibliography;

detailed Bibliographic Data can be found in Internet under www.dnb.de

First Edition August 2017

Translated from German by Susan Schuelke
Original title "Vom Vater" Publisher BoD Norderstedt

Production and Publisher:

BoD - Books on Demand, Norderstedt

ISBN 9783744895972

Contents

Introduction

"The Theology Jesus taught was completely Father-centred."

Quote from Prof. Dr. Knut Backhaus, German member of the Pontifical Biblical Commission.

Let us begin looking at a difficult theme with a joke:

Moses, an old man, and Jesus are playing golf together. Moses hits the ball first. He does a pretty good job - but it looks like the ball is going to fall in a pond. Suddenly he raises his golf club in the air, the water in the pond divides, the ball falls on the dry bottom of the pond and rolls out onto the Green. "Great Shot!", calls Jesus approvingly.

Jesus hits the ball with absolute perfection! The ball flies beautifully through the air - and lands on the Green, just a few centimetres from the hole. "Great Shot!" exclaims the old man.

The old man hits his ball again, but this time he is trembling, which makes the ball land next to a tree on the other side of the Green. Suddenly a squirrel appears, grabs the ball very quickly and runs away. Just at that second, out of nowhere, a big eagle flies down, snatches the squirrel with the ball and flies away. While being held by the eagle during his flight, the squirrel is able to let the ball fall - exactly into the golf hole! Jesus turns to the old man, pats him with admiration on his shoulder and says: " Great Shot, Papa!"

Many of us carry a similar picture of God around with us: Because we see him as an old feeble man, we don't trust him to carry the burdens of the world and ourselves in his hand nor positively influence our lives. Even worse, we think he has no idea of what is going on in the world. And if he does exist, he is far away from us, somewhere in heaven, far away from the dust of this world.

Or perhaps he is an unmerciful despot, who is not interested in helping us. Or we think he is a barbarian, who allows all the suffering in the world to continue.

This book is our attempt to explain how such a picture of God could develop and what Jesus really said about his Father. And which consequences this can have on his children.

It has been my, Heinrich, hearts wish for a long time to write about this. Many passages of this book are written as a dialogue, which we think is the best way to express God's wish to have a personal and very close relationship with each of us.

Hildegard and Heinrich Becker

Part 1: About Abba,

Preface

Father

What happens inside of you when you hear this word?

Father

Do positive feelings and thoughts well up in you?

Thoughts and memories of being protected and feeling secure?

Of loving experiences?

He took care of me, defended me, gave me gifts?

I could trust him, he appreciated me?

We did a lot with each other?

Father

Nothing happens inside me when I hear the word "Father".

I feel no connection to this word.

I never knew my father.

He was physically present, but otherwise not there.

He doesn't know me.

He left when my mother was pregnant with me.

He left us for another woman.

Father

I feel fear well up inside of me.

He was strict and not fair.

He didn't want any (more) children, I felt superfluous.

I had to protect my siblings and my mother.

He rejected me because I am of the wrong gender.

He rejected me because I didn't live up to his expectations.

Father

Rage develops in me.

He beat me.

He was often drunk.

He misused me.

He completely ruined my life.

In our book we want to show how to find the way to God, to point out who Jesus' Father was, how Jesus spoke of him in the New Testament. Jesus declares himself to be the only way to God the Father. And, in spite of this, the Father has disappeared from the realms of proclamation of the Gospel. Incorrect understanding has slyly found a way into proclamations, which have been corrected by different men and women in the last several years. Besides that, our biological father has a big influence upon our understanding of God, Jesus' Father. In many cases the own father stands in the way of a correct relationship to Abba, how Jesus named his Father.

That is the purpose of this book. And we share what we have personally experienced with our Father Abba.

God as Father?

God as Father!

How can God, who made heaven and earth, speak of himself as a Father?

No religion speaks about that! We only find these statements in the Bible. Gods are to be feared, one has to bribe them with offerings to please them or, at least, to avoid their wrath.

That is what happened with the God of the Bible, as we will see later.

And yet, he is spoken of as the Father in the Old Testament.

Actually we can really see the story of Creation as God's preparation of being a Father for his children, for whom he provides all of their needs.

Genesis 1:26

26 "Then God said, "Let us make mankind in our image, in our likeness,…"
After our image or appearance. Here, at the time of creation, we are not the same as God, but similar.
And he cares for his children: He comes into the Garden of Paradise every evening and talks with them about the day.[1] Also on the day when Adam and Eve sinned against him and brought sin into the world. They were still his children. In spite of their lack of trust and their doubts which were present.

The first time God speaks of himself as Father is in **1. Chronicles 22:10:**
 "He will build a temple for me. He will be my son, and I will be his father. His dynasty will rule Israel forever."

After God did not allow David to build a temple for him, God spoke to David about his son Salomon. He wanted to be a father for Salomon, who should be God's son. This is connected to his pledging to consolidate the throne of David over Israel. And, as we will later read, God endowed Salomon abundantly with

---

[1] Gen 3, 8a

13

wisdom and worldly riches.

A few chapters later when the building of the temple began, God repeated his Pledge.[2]

Now let us read about this in the Psalms:

First a statement of God about David:

„He will call out to me, 'You are my Father, my God, the Rock my Savior."[3]

In this verse the term Father is written before the term God. This order of terms shows that the relationship to our Father has precedence over speaking of him as God the Almighty One.

This description can be found in a Psalm written by David:

"As a father has compassion on his children, so the Lord has compassion on those who fear him; "[4]

David already wrote here about God's mercy: Like a father, he shows mercy to his children.

In Proverbs we can read the following verse, which isn't so easy to understand:

"...the Lord disciplines those he loves, as a father the son he delights in. "[5]

We prefer the Luther translation from 1984 even more:

"The Lord corrects those he loves, as parents correct a child of whom they are proud."

Upbringing and appreciation, or, in other words, liking someone, belong together. To love someone does not mean to accept and overlook everything that happens, but to keep one's goal for upbringing always in mind.

In Isaiah there is a verse which predicts Jesus' coming and his unity with his Father:

" For to us a child is born, to us a son is given, and the government will be on his shoulders. And he will be called Wonderful Counselor, Mighty God, Everlasting

---

[2] 1. Chr. 28, 6
[3] Psalm 89,26
[4] Psalm 103,13
[5] Proverbs 3, 12

Father, Prince of Peace. "[6]

Here we see God is spoken of as Father for the first time in Isaiah.[7]

"But you are our Father, though Abraham does not know us or Israel acknowledge us; you, Lord, are our Father, our Redeemer from of old is your name. ."

And again a few verses later:[8]

„Yet you, Lord, are our Father. We are the clay, you are the potter; we are all the work of your hand."

Now in Jeremia:

"Have you not just called to me: 'My Father, my friend from my youth,...."[9]

However, rather a reproach of God towards his people who deserted him. Also to be read in a few verses later:

„I myself said, 'How gladly would I treat you like my children and give you a pleasant land, the most beautiful inheritance of any nation.' I thought you would call me 'Father' and not turn away from following me.„[10]

In a later chapter of Jeremia we find similar words of God towards his people:

„They will come with weeping; they will pray as I bring them back. I will lead them beside streams of water on a level path where they will not stumble, because I am Israel's father, and Ephraim is my firstborn son. "

In Maleachi we found the last verses to this theme:

"Do we not all have one Father? Did not one God create us?11

Here we see that in the Old Testament God already spoke of himself as the Father of his children.

However, we see a radical change in the way Jesus spoke of his Father in the New Testament. Dr. Knut Backhaus, Professor for Catholic Theology at the Ludwig Maximillian University and German member of the Pontifical Biblical Commission said the following:

---

[6] Isaiah 9, 6

[7] Isa 63,16

[8] Isa 64, 8

[9] Jer 3, 4

[10] Jer,3,19

[11] Mal 2,10

"Jesus' theology was completely father-oriented".
To say it in a simpler way: Jesus' only concern was his Father and the commission his Father gave unto him.
From the multitude of Bible verses to this subject, we have reduced our list of verses found in the book of John:

John 1,14
The Word became flesh and made his dwelling among us. We have seen his glory, the glory of the one and only Son, who came from the Father, full of grace and truth.

John 1,18
No one has ever seen God, but the one and only Son, who is himself God and is in closest relationship with the Father, has made him known.

John 2,16
To those who sold doves he said, "Get these out of here! Stop turning my Father's house into a market!"

John 3:35
The Father loves the Son and has placed everything in his hands.

John 4, 21 + 23
"Woman," Jesus replied, "believe me, a time is coming when you will worship the Father neither on this mountain nor in Jerusalem. Yet a time is coming and has now come when the true worshipers will worship the Father in the Spirit and in truth, for they are the kind of worshipers the Father seeks.

John 5,17-23
In his defense Jesus said to them, "My Father is always at his work to this very day, and I too am working." For this reason they tried all the more to kill him; not only was he breaking the Sabbath, but he was even calling God his own Father, making himself equal with God. Jesus gave them this answer: "Very truly I tell you, the Son can do nothing by himself; he can do only what he sees his Father doing, because whatever the Father does the Son also does. For the

Father loves the Son and shows him all he does. Yes, and he will show him even greater works than these, so that you will be amazed.1 For just as the Father raises the dead and gives them life, even so the Son gives life to whom he is pleased to give it. Moreover, the Father judges no one, but has entrusted all judgment to the Son, that all may honor the Son just as they honor the Father. Whoever does not honor the Son does not honor the Father, who sent him.

John 5, 26
For as the Father has life in himself, so he has granted the Son also to have life in himself.

John 5,30
By myself I can do nothing; I judge only as I hear, and my judgment is just, for I seek not to please myself but him who sent me.

John 5, 36-37
I have testimony weightier than that of John. For the works that the Father has given me to finish—the very works that I am doing—testify that the Father has sent me. And the Father who sent me has himself testified concerning me. You have never heard his voice nor seen his form,

John 5, 43 + 45
I have come in my Father's name, and you do not accept me; but if someone else comes in his own name, you will accept him.
But do not think I will accuse you before the Father. Your accuser is Moses, on whom your hopes are set.

John 6,27
Do not work for food that spoils, but for food that endures to eternal life, which the Son of Man will give you. For on him God the Father has placed his seal of approval.

John 6,32
Jesus said to them, "Very truly I tell you, it is not Moses who has given you the

bread from heaven, but it is my Father who gives you the true bread from heaven.

John 6:37
All those the Father gives me will come to me, and whoever comes to me I will never drive away.

John 6, 40-46
For my Father's will is that everyone who looks to the Son and believes in him shall have eternal life, and I will raise them up at the last day." At this the Jews there began to grumble about him because he said, "I am the bread that came down from heaven." They said, "Is this not Jesus, the son of Joseph, whose father and mother we know? How can he now say, 'I came down from heaven'?" "Stop grumbling among yourselves," Jesus answered. "No one can come to me unless the Father who sent me draws them, and I will raise them up at the last day. It is written in the Prophets: 'They will all be taught by God.'4 Everyone who has heard the Father and learned from him comes to me. No one has seen the Father except the one who is from God; only he has seen the Father.

John 6,57
Just as the living Father sent me and I live because of the Father, so the one who feeds on me will live because of me.

John 6,65
 And he added, "This is the very reason I told you that no people can come to me unless the Father makes it possible for them to do so.

John 8,16-19
But if I do judge, my decisions are true, because I am not alone. I stand with the Father, who sent me. In your own Law it is written that the testimony of two witnesses is true. I am one who testifies for myself; my other witness is the Father, who sent me." Then they asked him, "Where is your father?" "You do not know me or my Father," Jesus replied. "If you knew me, you would know my Father also."

John 8,27+28

They did not understand that he was telling them about his Father.
So Jesus said, "When you have lifted up1 the Son of Man, then you will know
that I am he and that I do nothing on my own but speak just what the Father has
taught me."

John 8,38

 I am telling you what I have seen in the Father's presence, and you are doing
what you have heard from your father.

John 8,41-42

You are doing the works of your own father.
"We are not illegitimate children," they protested. "The only Father we have is
God himself."
Jesus said to them, "If God were your Father, you would love me, for I have
come here from God. I have not come on my own; God sent me.

John 8,49

„I am not possessed by a demon," said Jesus, "but I honor my Father and you
dishonor me."

John 8,54

 Jesus replied, "If I glorify myself, my glory means nothing. My Father, whom you
claim as your God, is the one who glorifies me."

John 10,14 + 15

I am the good shepherd; I know my sheep and my sheep know me, just as the
Father knows me and I know the Father—and I lay down my life for the sheep.

John 10,17 + 18

The reason my Father loves me is that I lay down my life—only to take it up
again. No one takes it from me, but I lay it down of my own accord. I have
authority to lay it down and authority to take it up again. This command I
received from my Father.

John 10,25

Jesus answered, "I did tell you, but you do not believe. The works I do in my Father's name testify about me.

John 10, 29 + 30 + 32
My Father, who has given them to me, is greater than all; no one can snatch them out of my Father's hand. I and the Father are one.
But Jesus said to them, "I have shown you many good works from the Father. For which of these do you stone me?"

John 10:36-38
What about the one whom the Father set apart as his very own and sent into the world? Why then do you accuse me of blasphemy because I said, 'I am God's Son'? Do not believe me unless I do the works of my Father. But if I do them, even though you do not believe me, believe the works, that you may know and understand that the Father is in me, and I in the Father."

John 11, 41
So they took away the stone. Then Jesus looked up and said, "Father, I thank you that you have heard me.

John 12, 26-28
Whoever serves me must follow me; and where I am, my servant also will be. My Father will honor the one who serves me.
Now my soul is troubled, and what shall I say? 'Father, save me from this hour'? No, it was for this very reason I came to this hour.
Father, glorify your name!" Then a voice came from heaven, "I have glorified it, and will glorify it again."

John 12, 49 + 50
For I did not speak on my own, but the Father who sent me commanded me to say all that I have spoken. I know that his command leads to eternal life. So whatever I say is just what the Father has told me to say.

John 13:1 + 3
It was just before the Passover Festival. Jesus knew that the hour had come for

him to leave this world and go to the Father. Having loved his own who were in the world, he loved them to the end. Jesus knew that the Father had put all things under his power, and that he had come from God and was returning to God.

John 14:2
My Father's house has many rooms; if that were not so, would I have told you that I am going there to prepare a place for you?

John 14:6-13
Jesus answered, "I am the way and the truth and the life. No one comes to the Father except through me.
If you really know me, you will know my Father as well. From now on, you do know him and have seen him.
Philip said, "Lord, show us the Father and that will be enough for us."
Jesus answered: "Don't you know me, Philip, even after I have been among you such a long time? Anyone who has seen me has seen the Father. How can you say, 'Show us the Father'?
Don't you believe that I am in the Father, and that the Father is in me? The words I say to you I do not speak on my own authority. Rather, it is the Father, living in me, who is doing his work.
Believe me when I say that I am in the Father and the Father is in me; or at least believe on the evidence of the works themselves.
Very truly I tell you, whoever believes in me will do the works I have been doing, and they will do even greater things than these, because I am going to the Father.
And I will do whatever you ask in my name, so that the Father may be glorified in the Son."

John 14,16
And I will ask the Father, and he will give you another advocate to help you and be with you forever.

John 14, 20-28
On that day you will realize that I am in my Father, and you are in me, and I am in you. Whoever has my commands and keeps them is the one who loves me.

The one who loves me will be loved by my Father, and I too will love them and show myself to them."

Then Judas (not Judas Iscariot) said, "But, Lord, why do you intend to show yourself to us and not to the world?"

Jesus replied, "Anyone who loves me will obey my teaching. My Father will love them, and we will come to them and make our home with them.

Anyone who does not love me will not obey my teaching. These words you hear are not my own; they belong to the Father who sent me. All this I have spoken while still with you. But the Advocate, the Holy Spirit, whom the Father will send in my name, will teach you all things and will remind you of everything I have said to you. Peace I leave with you; my peace I give you. I do not give to you as the world gives. Do not let your hearts be troubled and do not be afraid. "You heard me say, 'I am going away and I am coming back to you.' If you loved me, you would be glad that I am going to the Father, for the Father is greater than I."

John 14, 31
but he comes so that the world may learn that I love the Father and do exactly what my Father has commanded me."Come now; let us leave."

John 15, 1
I am the true vine, and my Father is the gardener.

John 15, 8-10
This is to my Father's glory, that you bear much fruit, showing yourselves to be my disciples.

As the Father has loved me, so have I loved you. Now remain in my love. If you keep my commands, you will remain in my love, just as I have kept my Father's commands and remain in his love.

John 15, 15 - 16
I no longer call you servants, because a servant does not know his master's business. Instead, I have called you friends, for everything that I learned from my Father I have made known to you. You did not choose me, but I chose you and appointed you so that you might go and bear fruit—fruit that will last—and so that whatever you ask in my name the Father will give you.

John 15, 23 - 24
Whoever hates me hates my Father as well. If I had not done among them the works no one else did, they would not be guilty of sin. As it is, they have seen, and yet they have hated both me and my Father.

John 15, 26
When the Advocate comes, whom I will send to you from the Father—the Spirit of truth who goes out from the Father—he will testify about me.

John 16,3
They will do such things because they have not known the Father or me.

John 16:10
about righteousness, because I am going to the Father, where you can see me no longer;

John 16, 15
All that belongs to the Father is mine. That is why I said the Spirit will receive from me what he will make known to you."

John 16, 17
At this, some of his disciples said to one another, "What does he mean by saying, 'In a little while you will see me no more, and then after a little while you will see me,' and 'Because I am going to the Father'?"

John 16, 23
In that day you will no longer ask me anything. Very truly I tell you, my Father will give you whatever you ask in my name.

John 16, 25 - 28
Though I have been speaking figuratively, a time is coming when I will no longer use this kind of language but will tell you plainly about my Father. In that day you will ask in my name. I am not saying that I will ask the Father on your behalf. No, the Father himself loves you because you have loved me and have believed that I came from God. I came from the Father and entered the world; now I am

leaving the world and going back to the Father.

John 16, 32
A time is coming and in fact has come when you will be scattered, each to your own home. You will leave me all alone. Yet I am not alone, for my Father is with me.

John 17, 5
And now, Father, glorify me in your presence with the glory I had with you before the world began.

John 17, 11
I will remain in the world no longer, but they are still in the world, and I am coming to you. Holy Father, protect them by the power of your name, the name you gave me, so that they may be one as we are one.

John 17, 21
That all of them may be one, Father, just as you are in me and I am in you. May they also be in us so that the world may believe that you have sent me.

John 17, 24-25
Father, I want those you have given me to be with me where I am, and to see my glory, the glory you have given me because you loved me before the creation of the world. Righteous Father, though the world does not know you, I know you, and they know that you have sent me.

John 18, 11
Jesus commanded Peter, "Put your sword away! Shall I not drink the cup the Father has given me?

John 20, 17
Jesus said, "Do not hold on to me, for I have not yet ascended to the Father. Go instead to my brothers and tell them, 'I am ascending to my Father and your Father, to my God and your God."

John 20, 21
Again Jesus said, "Peace be with you! As the Father has sent me, I am sending

you."

It is overwhelming how often Jesus spoke of his Father in the Gospel of John. More than 110 times! That was Jesus' greatest desire. What an intimate relationship they shared!
It is the same in the other Gospels.
One verse of scripture we have already quoted means so much to us that we want to repeat it again:[12]
„Moreover, the Father judges no one, but has entrusted all judgment to the Son."
God surrendered to his son, Jesus Christ, the sovereign power and authority to reign and judge with truth and righteousness in order for himself to be **FULLY** our Father! Jesus will sit on the Throne of Judgment. God the Father will remain our Father.

And yet, God the Father has disappeared from the proclaimed word.

Why?

That is what the next chapter is about.

---

[12] John 5,22

Jesus' Father disappears

Let us take a look at the Proclamation of the Bible as it takes place in churches today, not considering the differences in the many confessions. In our opinion, the percentage of how often God, Jesus and the Holy Spirit are proclaimed is alarming. Jesus' is mentioned approximately 93% of the time, the Holy Spirit only 5%, but God the Father is mentioned even less - 2% of the time!
It is not our purpose to degrade Jesus' proclamations; instead, we are concerned about the following words of Jesus: „ Jesus answered him, "I am the way, the truth, and the life; no one comes to the Father except by me."[13] Jesus' intent here was to direct their attention to his Father, who was his main point of interest. More about this later. The big question is WHY did God the Father disappear from the proclamation in churches?

The history of the development in the early churches.

At the end of the first and beginning of the second centuries, the heathen philosophy of the Greek philosophers Plato and Aristotle influenced the thinking of early Christianity. They described the character of their gods with the Greek word „apotheia", which is the definition of Greek gods (Apothee). These gods are very distant; there is no way to reach them. They are unable to love or to have compassion because they exist in spheres above our world. They are only involved with themselves and are not interested in human beings. There is one exception: very beautiful young girls.
In the ancient world of the Greeks and Romans no compassion, no love, no humanitarian values existed. Instead, the Greek ideal for all people was worshipped, which was „A healthy spirit in a healthy Body." The disabled, the sick, the weak, those who were not capable of taking part in military campaigns, the simple - they were of no value in heathen Greek Philosophy. Again, there was the exception of girls who were young and beautiful.

The heathen concept of God, along with the Greek ideal of humans, made it impossible to understand who Jesus' true Father was, although Jesus' life

---

[13] Joh. 14 ,6

exemplified to his disciples who God was. Through the influence of Greek thinking upon early Christianity, Jesus' Father was reduced to a distant god who did not suffer with us, did not love us when we were guilty, did not offer his help when we were lost or when others had misused us, who looked at us without any interest when our bodies, minds and spirits were sick nor when we struggled and were plagued. In the Theology of the church he was a God who resided in heaven, unreachable for sinful people who could not see themselves as beloved children of God. And these children are the ones who fear God's anger. This heathen idea influenced the early Christian theology and had great influence on the understanding of who God is, even up to this day.

At the beginning of the 4th century Konstantin lifted Christianity out of its low-class position up to the position of a State Religion in the Roman Empire, which was the beginning of the dependence of the Church upon the state and society. The state, i.e. the Roman Empire, bestowed many privileges upon the Church in order to be able to take advantage of its moral and religious values. For the Empire, which was beginning to fall apart, needed the organizing and unifying power of the church. Bishops became worldly judges. This is when the church of believers became a religion; they were far away from Jesus' love and his Father's love for his children. God's children became subject to the ruling leaders; they were controlled, judged, found guilty and persecuted. The focus of the State Church was upon commandments, laws and teachings, which were to be obeyed. The early church completely lost the teaching about the loving Father. The Church wanted to enjoy some of the privileges and structures of the state also, in order to have power and control during times of false teachings. During the Middle Ages, at the time of the Inquisition, which was actually a good idea in that those accused of heresy were first interrogated instead of being executed, false teachings had reached its peak. Even scientific progress was seen as an attack on the infallibility of the church and was unmercifully persecuted. Nothing was said about a loving Father who, in order to be with his children, came into the world through his son Jesus Christ.

Worldly influences invade the church

At the beginning of the 19th Century the Industrialization took fathers away from their families, since the working world brutally tore families apart. Today many fathers are not am example to their children of how to master the difficulties of life, but have become a person with authority, who is to be feared upon arrival at home and with whom a close relationship is not possible. These children are not able to later identify themselves with their father which causes a feeling of desolation and aloneness. Subsequently, the impression is given of a weak father, who is incapable and upon whom one cannot depend. Philosophers and Theologians have given God this attribute which, because of the no-existent God of the 19. century, the „God is dead" Ideology of the 20 century began, at cost of millions of people in Russia under Stalin and in Germany under Hitler, their lives.

Along with the destructive influences beginning in the 19th century came also destruction caused by the last two World Wars. Many fathers never came back home. The fatherless society was born.

And today?
Before we begin to talk about our heavenly father, we must talk about our own fathers and step-fathers. There have been too many of them over a long period of time who never learned to take over their responsibility of caring for their wives and children and to fulfill the teachings of Paul ,as written in Ephesians: „Husbands, love your wives just as Christ loved the church and gave his life for it.."[14]

Separations, divorces and the emotional absence of fathers because of work, television and computer, soccer and other sports and also alcohol and sexual relationships, have hindered many fathers from being able to build up close emotional and trustworthy relationships with their children.

Since there is no substitute for a Father-Son relationship in our lives, many of us live with feelings of abandonment and loneliness. And we transfer the negative experiences we had without a father or with a father who was present but was emotionally absent, upon God.

What remains are false, twisted ideas about God who can only be seen as

---

[14] Eph 5,25

omnipotent, omniscient, omnipresent, as Lord over life and death. In the best case he is fair, an impartial judge who helps the good and the weak, punishes those who are bad, rewards pious performance and gives those who are eager long healthy lives.

I, Hildegard, grew up with these twisted, cold ideas stamped upon my soul. When I gave my life to Christ, false understanding of who God was did not change. Not until many years later did I find out:

The truth about the person of God wasn't explained in the teachings of the church; instead he was again, as in past history, described as an ambiguous, equivocal God of the Old Testament. He created mankind to have fellowship with him and even sent his own Son as Savior and Lord into the world but how did this knowledge about God influence people? They became fearful of God. Even though he created us to have fellowship with him and sent his Son into the world to show us the way to Himself, each person was punished at the end of their life with death. This fear of God is worse than the fear of death. The following sentence spoken by my father-in-law many years ago was very disturbing:
„Whoever wants to be as close to God as possible in eternity must put forth great effort to lead a holy life. Only few people ever achieve this."

This twisted and false picture of God became a heavy burden: God is never pleased, only the best are allowed to look at him from a distance. I will never be able to reach this holiness and look at him face to face.

As I was trained to strive for achieving and because of the very difficult experiences I had with my own father, I wasn't able to accept God's love for me. My desire for love and acceptance was so deep that I became ill at the age of 40.

Unsatisfied desires

These unsatisfied desires have to do with what God spoke to his already created world at the time of Creation:
„Then God said, "And now we will make human beings; they will be like us and

resemble us." (Genesis 1,26).

We are created in the image of God, modeled according to his being, similar to him in our humanness. But mankind lost this similarity to God's being. When did that happen? When we turned our backs on him, wanting, through our own efforts and our own power, to be like him. Because of this fatal mistake, we are plagued all of our life with the unsatisfied desire to personify the divine attributes of God, the loving, ever caring Father, which God had already given to us. What are the basic desires and needs of each of us?

The first basic need is Love. This can best be explained with the example of the young, naive and trusting child, who asks its parents ."Do you love me?" If this question is not answered with an unmistakable „Yes!", then the child begins to ask itself „What do I have to do to be loved?"

We were created out of love and made to love. Receiving, giving and showing love are basic needs of every child. A lack of love cripples our souls and there, where it hurts the most, becomes hardened. We build up a wall around ourselves to protect us.

The second basic need is appreciation and esteem of who I am. Not what I have achieved or my good behavior.

Because these basic needs of many children were never met, as adults they seek to still their unsatisfied desires through success, power, sex and wealth. Inside many successful men there is the „inner young child" which has the never-ending need to prove to their fathers what great guys they are! And many daughters, who have hungered for the love and approval of their fathers, end up in wrong partnerships and dependencies.

Today many people classify their own freedom to be more important than a personal relationship with God and miss out on receiving God's appreciation of them.

The third basic need is to find out what the meaning of life is. To be given the answer where I came from and where I am going. What my purpose in this world is, what I was created for. These human existential questions were originally answered through the loving fellowship with God the Father and through his commission to the people he created to increase themselves and to build up and protect the earth.

Without God, self-realization, the desire for romantic love and the fulfillment found through one's own personal achievements, which can be a remembrance of one's own successes even after death, were goals to live for.

The fourth basic need is for safety and the knowledge of where I belong, where my roots are, where my home is. Our greatest desire, never changing until this day, is to be at the original place where God planned for us to be, in the Garden of Paradise.

Karl Marx wanted to create the Garden Of Paradise by human means. You know better than I do what became of this plan. Socialism and communism were the human efforts to build the Kingdom of God's Peace upon earth.

But what was God our Father's intention?
And how can we return to the place he wanted us to be?

God the Father and I.

What is the great news in the Bible about God our Father? The big headlines read:

He wants to have a personal relationship with us. As we will see later; he wants even more than that!

Let's take a close look to read what the Bible has to say about this.

He wanted me.

In the book of Isaiah is written:

„But now, this is what the Lord says— he who created you, Jacob, he who formed you, Israel."[15]

Substitute the names Jacob and Israel with our names and see how the meaning of the text changes: God the Father created you and made you. But that is not all! He speaks to you! The most important verse in the Bible!

In this verse we read further: Fear **not!** One of the most important declarations in the Bible. When a very important message is going to be spoken by a Prophet, God the Father, or an Angel, they begin by saying: Fear not!

The clearest examples of this are the declaration of the conception of Jesus to Mary and Joseph[16] as well as the good tidings about the birth of Jesus[17]!

Religion continually says: Be fearful of the almighty God, of Hell and Punishment from whomever it comes.

God's Adversary says: Fear God!

God the Father says: Fear **not!** I longed for you!

When did He long for me?

Not when my parent's decided to have a child, not when I was conceived, not when we were born. Nor when we were somehow already here!

In Ephesians we can read: „Even before the world was made, God had already

---

[15] Jes 43, 1a

[16] Matth 1, 20; Luke 1,30

[17] Luke 2,10

chosen us to be."[18] That is really a very long time ago; according to how we figure out the number of years, probably around 5800 years or several billion years. And all this time God the Father was thinking about his child. Which talents and abilities he would lay in his child, what it will look like, how much he will love it. Which very special relationship he wants to have with his child. How beautiful it will be when it sits in his lap. And now it is here. Now YOU are here. And he is waiting to begin a relationship with you if you don't have one yet with him, or to intensify the relationship you do already have.

In the Psalms we read: „You saw me before I was born. The days allotted to me had all been recorded in your book, before any of them ever began."[19] What this text means is that I was premeditated, all the days of my life were thought out. NOT predetermined! God gave us a free will. He wants to have a relationship with us, from the time of our birth into all eternity. Eternity!!

When does eternal life begin? Not after we die; that is a completely false interpretation. John explained this very exactly in his Epistle: „Now this is eternal life: that they know you, the only true God, and Jesus Christ, whom you have sent."[20] That means at the moment that I commit my life to Jesus and to follow the way my Father leads me, my eternal life has begun! More to this in the chapter „Eternal Life".

He knows me by my name.

He is the God who knows me by my name! In Isaiah is written: „I have summoned you by your name - you are mine."[21] In biblical times the father decided on the name or at least confirmed the name. Let's take Zechariah as an example. He gave his son the name John and not Zechariah, which was the rule of tradition at that time.[22] God our Father doesn't only know us, but he knows us by name. Every single person who has ever lived from the beginning of time he knows by name.

Who doesn't know who our Federal President of Germany is? Were he to ring our door bell and enter our house, we would immediately know: That's him!!

---

[18] Eph 1,4
[19] Psalm 139,16 Good News Bible
[20] John 17,3
[21] Isa 43,1b
[22] Luke 1,63

But does he know you? Not including the people he already knows, he would definitely not know who you are. He has no idea who you are nor knows that you and I exist. And certainly doesn't know our names.

But God the Father knows the name of the trillions of people who live on this earth! And also of those who have already died. Everyone. By Name.

And even more!

God our Father knows the number of hairs upon each of our heads! [23] We have a household book in which we write down how much money we have given out per day – perhaps we make 2 to 3 entries per day and that is something that takes time to keep up with. And with our hair, we lose between 50 to 100 hairs per day, which will be replaced by new hairs. That would be impossible to write down and keep up with each day. And yet God our Father knows the exact number! Even big Secret Service Organizations cannot do that, despite of Big Data!

And even more again!

In Psalm 56 is the following verse: „You keep track of all my sorrows. You have collected all my tears in your bottle. You have recorded each one in your book. „ [24]

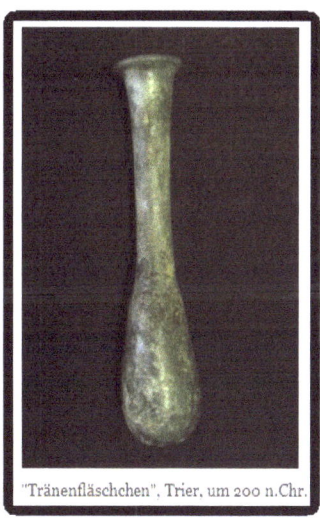

Several years ago when on vacation with our trailer in the South of France, we were standing one day somewhere in a field and the owner came up to us and invited us to his home. During the visit he showed us a roman gravesite which he had found and also a small beautiful glass vessel . He explained that in the vessel all the tears of the family members had been collected and laid in the grave of the deceased.

God our Father collects all of our tears because he suffers with us and these shed tears are very precious to him.

"Tränenfläschchen", Trier, um 200 n.Chr.

Even Jesus needed his Father's confirmation that he knew him. „And a voice

[23] Luke 12,7
[24] Psalm 56,8

from heaven said, "You are my dearly loved Son, and you bring me great joy." [25]
The human side of him needed that, even though he was the true God.
And the same is true for us: You are my beloved son; you are my beloved
daughter, you bring me great joy. You are the children I so longed for. I love you!

We give each of our children a first name. That is their identification, not to be
mistaken of in our family. And we have a family name, which embeds us in our
family history. We did not come out of Nowhere, but from a family. However
our true names are: „ Prince or Princess of our Father." We are heavenly royalty!
God our Father has adopted us, we belong to his family. From the beginning of
time.

He knows all the details of my life.

This is where we have to look at the major difficulties which have come up. Why?
Because of the way we were brought up, our characteristics or our religion, we
have learned to see God as a Policeman or Santa Claus. And of course attached
to us is a long list of sins, of which he accuses us: When we have failed, where
and when we have sinned.

First of all I must clear up a wrong understanding of the word „sin". According to
the Bible sin is not a deed but is a condition. The condition is that we are
separated from God the Father. And that is why God hates sin – the condition
which separates us from him! But he loves the sinner, those who are separated
from him. That is why Jesus loved most of all to sit among the sinners! And
exactly that enraged the religious leaders of his day. Those who made great
efforts to do everything right for God were the ones Jesus corrected the most
often. The Crux of the matter is this: The important thing is NOT to do
everything right, but to be a child of God the Father, not to become one. We are
already that! In Psalm 139:1-18 we can read what he thinks about us:[26]

1 You have searched me, Lord, and you know me.
2 You know when I sit and when I rise; you perceive my thoughts from afar.

---

[25] Mark 1, 11
[26] Psalm 139, 1-18

3 You discern my going out and my lying down; you are familiar with all my ways.

4 Before a word is on my tongue you, Lord, know it completely.

5 You hem me in behind and before, and you lay your hand upon me.

6 Such knowledge is too wonderful for me, too lofty for me to attain.

7 Where can I go from your Spirit? Where can I flee from your presence?

8 If I go up to the heavens, you are there; if I make my bed in the depths, you are there.[27]

9 If I rise on the wings of the dawn, if I settle on the far side of the sea,

10 even there your hand will guide me, your right hand will hold me fast.

11 If I say, "Surely the darkness will hide me and the light become night around me,"

12 even the darkness will not be dark to you; the night will shine like the day, for darkness is as light to you.

13 For you created my inmost being; you knit me together in my mother's womb.

14 I praise you because I am fearfully and wonderfully made; your works are wonderful, I know that full well.

15 My frame was not hidden from you when I was made in the secret place, when I was woven together in the depths of the earth.

16 Your eyes saw my unformed body; all the days ordained for me were written in your book before one of them came to be.

17 How precious to me are your thoughts, God! How vast is the sum of them!

18 Were I to count them, they would outnumber the grains of sand— when I awake, I am still with you.

Is this positive or negative? Is this the sentence of my punishment? NO! This is pure astonishment, thanks and amazement about God the Father.

The last verse speaks of God's thoughts, which outnumber the grains of sand. There are more stars in space than there are grains of sand all over the world. We just read [28] that there are probably more galaxies than grains of sand. And

---

[27] In the German text the Hebrew word „Scheol" is used for describing the underworld of the dead; in the English translation, NIV, Scheol means the depths.

[28] Frankfurter Allgemeine Zeitung pageN2 as of 27.07.2016

yet God knows all the stars by name! [29] That means that he could give every grain of sand a name.

Whoever can do that, knows who I am. And we are more than just a grain of sand, we are his beloved children!

We can talk to him. He is willing to be on my level and he lifts me up to the heights of his level.

Like the Papa carrying his 3-year old child on his arm.

He takes care of me.

In Isaiah we read:[30]

„... because you are precious to me. You are honored, and I love you.„ Perhaps not exactly as you expected. Quite often we have very exact ideas of how God should help us right away. This reminds me of little children who so often definitely want something without thinking about the consequences nor the impact of having it. We will talk more about this in the chapter „Becoming a Child".

Other promises of God:

For God has said, "I will never fail you. I will never abandon you." [31]

Even if it looks like he would abandon us or our past experiences hinder us from believing him.

In Isaiah God speaks very clearly to Israel:[32]

„Listen to me, you descendants of Jacob, all the remnant of the people of Israel, you whom I have upheld since your birth, and have carried since you were born. Even to your old age and gray hairs I am he, I am he who will sustain you. I have made you and I will carry you; I will sustain you and I will rescue you."

---

[29] Isa 40,26
[30] Isa 43,4a
[31] Heb 15,5
[32] Isa 46, 3-4

In the very beautiful poem written by Margret Fishback Powers, she asks God: Where were you during the most troublesome times of my life, where I see only one set of footprints in the sand? And God answers: When you saw only one set of footprints, it was then that I carried you!

Which name did Jesus call his Father? ABBA. This word can hardly be found in the New Testament. The reason is that there is no substantial translation for the Aramaic word Abba in the Greek language. There we only find πατέρα or the word the Romans used, Patriarch. He had the sole right to decide upon the fate of his family members and to sell, kill or abandon his children. The word ABBA is the childlike, trusting name used, the syllable most babies speak first and can be compared to the German name Papa. God wants us to call him by this name! Even your own childlike syllables are sufficient to talk with your Heavenly Father, the Creator of the Universe!

He loves what he sees.

Sometimes we think that God looks disapprovingly upon us, but that is absolutely wrong! He loves us, even when we have turned our backs upon him. In 1. John we read:
„This is real love—not that we loved God, but that he loved us and sent his Son as a sacrifice to take away our sins.[33] In order to lead us out of our separation from him. God loves the sinner and hates sin. If Jesus died for our sins, then what is left of the previous sentence is: God loves the sinner.

We read in Romans:[34]
„But God showed his great love for us by sending Christ to die for us while we were still sinners.“

---

[33] 1.John 4, 10
[34] Rom 5,8

And in Zephaniah we can also read: (New International Version):[35]
„The Lord your God is with you, the Mighty Warrior who saves. He will take great delight in you; in his love he will no longer rebuke you, but will rejoice over you with singing." [36]
Matthias Hoffmann once said: „God loves us as we are, but he doesn't leave us that way. He wants to draw us out of the distance we have put between us and bring us closer to himself."

He has a purpose for my life and he leads me there.
The first human for whom God the Father had a purpose was Adam.[37]
„So the LORD God formed from the ground all the wild animals and all the birds of the sky. He brought them to the man to see what he would call them, and the man chose a name for each one. He gave names to all the livestock, all the birds of the sky, and all the wild animals."
The fulfilling of Adam's purpose began with God the Father and Adam working together. God had the idea and Adam was to help. This is the order of events when God begins to work with us: He has the idea and we are called to help him. It is comparable to the first time our young child wants to help set the table by carrying the plates and we look with anxiety, seeing what could go wrong. That is about what happens with Abba when he shows us his purpose for our lives. But sadly, the order of events is often turned around: WE have the idea and want Abba to help us. Sometimes he goes along with us for awhile until we reach the point of not knowing what our next step should be and then ask him to lead us. Abba, by the way, is the only One who can make something good out of our mistakes. And he does that. The best example for us is Joseph in the Old Testament and how God, in one day, took him out of his life of slavery and imprisonment and set him upon the throne as the most important person after Pharaoh. This is the way God realized his purpose in Joseph's life.[38]
Adam's job, or commission, was tremendous! No scientist today would be able to do that, which he had to do. Finding a name for each of the 160 000 species of butterflies is gigantic. Even more than that, we don't even know what 80% of

---

[35] Zeph 3, 17
[36] Matthias Hoffmann is director of the Father Heart Movement
www.vaterherz.org
[37] Gen 2,19-20a
[38] Gen 37 and the following chapter

the animals are, which live in the Deep Sea, which means that not even biologists have a name for them. But Adam was able to fulfill his job. This is a definite sign of how much was lost for all of humanity when Adam had to leave Paradise.

God the Father has a Commission for each of us. Just as Prophets in the Old Testament and Disciples in the New Testament had.

You have a job, you are not a Nobody. That was made clear when you were called by God. And yet, God has to tell us what our job is. Not something that we perhaps really want to do. Or what seems to be the best thing for the moment. Or what others want us to do.

In Psalm 139[39] is written: „Every day of my life was recorded in your book." God the Creator thought about me, planned all the days of MY life. Just for me. From the beginning of time, as we have already seen.

And he meditated and planned in detail. The best interpretation of this was written by Franz von Sales[40] (short passage)

„He (God the Father) looked exactly upon this job for you before he sent it to you, looked at this job with his omniscient eyes, planned it with his godly understanding, examined it with his wise righteousness, warmed it in his arms of love, held it with both hands to see if it was a millimeter too big or a milligram too heavy. He blessed it in his holiest of holy names, anointed it through and through with his mercy and blessed it with the sweet smells of his comfort. And then he looked again at you and your courage and sent this as a Greeting from God to you, as a gift of his all merciful love."

But God wants my consent. That I say „Yes" to my job. Out of trust to him. Trusting him daily. And that is not easy for us, as we will soon see.

ABBA-God wants to express himself through you.

God our Father wants to show the world who he is through you. Something that

---

[39] Psalm 139,16 Hermann Menge Translation, 11. Edition, Württembergische Bibelanstalt

[40] Franz von Sales was a Bishop of Geneva and resided in Annecy, founded an Order, Mystical writer, church teachings in the 16th Century.

only you can show the world. He needs you for this. 7 billion people are not even enough to explain everything that Abba God is.

HE needs you.

To tell the world something that ONLY you can tell.

If you refuse, then this message for the world will remain unheard and unseen. I do not want to put you under pressure, but want you to know how unique you are.

Paul de Lagarde [41] expressed it this way:

„Every person is a very special thought of God."

And very ingenious, which is the theme of a song written by Paul Janz, German lyrics by Juergen Werth: (Chorus)

He wanted you, you weren't created by chance, it wasn't a mood of nature,

It doesn't matter if you sing your life song in minor or in major.

You are a thought of God, a very unique one.

That is you, that is the Clou, yes the Clou. Yes, that is you.

God wants to be a Father.

Here are several verses from the Old Testament which speak of God the Father:

Deuteronomy 32, 6b: „Is he not your Father, your Creator, who made you and formed you?"

2. Sam 7, 14 spoken to Salomon: „I will be his father, and he will be my son."

1. Chronicles 17, 13: God to David: „I will be his father, and he will be my son."

Psalm 68, 5 David: „A father to the fatherless, a defender of widows, is God in his holy dwelling."

Psalm 89, 26 David:"You are my Father, my God, the Rock my Savior.' "

Psalm 103, 13 David: As a father is kind to his children, so the Lord is kind to those who honor him."

Isaiah 63, 16   „But you are our Father, though Abraham does not know us or Israel acknowledge us; you, Lord, are our Father, our Redeemer from of old is your name. ."

---

[41]Paul de Lagarde was a German cultural philosopher and orientalist in the 19th century.

Jeremiah 31, 9 „They will come with weeping; they will pray as I bring them back. I will lead them beside streams of water on a level path where they will not stumble, because I am Israel's father, and Ephraim is my firstborn son."
Malachi 2, 10 „Do we not all have one Father? Did not one God create us?"

How can we have this type relationship with our Father?

We have to become a child to enter the Kingdom of God. We will learn more about that in the chapter **Being a child of God the Father.**

But there is one hurdle we have to overcome:

When we talk about God's Father ship, about Abba, it could be that some of us have a problem in our relationship to him. And that might be:
My and your earthly Father.
However you experienced your earthly father will be the way you imagine and see Abba.
If he was good and trustworthy, God will be the same way.
I thank God for the fathers who were this way to their children.
Also Christian fathers fail here. Our three children told me very clearly in which situations they did not feel loved, I did not respect what they wanted, I did not see their needs, when I put them down. We spoke about that and I asked them for forgiveness. And they forgave me. That was a wonderful moment in our relationship.

If your earthly father disregarded you, you will expect God to do the same with you.
If he left you and gave you away, God will do the same with you.
If he went over boundaries that only belonged to you, God will do the same.
If he misjudged you, then God will do the same.
If he ever beat you, then God will also punish you.

But that is not the truth:

God Abba is different. He wanted you to be his son or daughter. We hope that we have been able to make this clear to you in this chapter.
Because God Abba wanted you, he will always stand by you and believe in you!
Most of all in the situation in which you were born and grew up.

Parents can decide if they want to have children. When the children are there, there is no way to dissolve the relationship. We will always be the children of our parents. Whether or not they knew us, wanted us, rejected us, our relationship was good or bad – we will always be, forever, the children of our parents.

Abba Father loves you and wants to show you who he is as Father, but it could be that your earthly father, who perhaps didn't love you or left you, is in the way of Abba Father.

It could be that you had a loving father, but the Christian church you attended preached a punishing God, who, like a policeman, saw everything you did and even threatened to send you to hell if you sinned. Perhaps these fears lie very deeply anchored within you. But that is religion and has nothing to with Abba God!
Religion says: Be fearful! Abba says: Fear not!
This is written more than ten times in the Gospels of the New Testament. Very often the words God spoke to his people in the Old Testament began with „Fear not!"

How can we give up the lies we took for granted and live the truth of who God is and we are?
By forgiving. And that is not easy.
Two verses in Hesekiel[42] have become very important for me:
„The people of the land practice extortion and commit robbery; they oppress the poor and needy and mistreat the foreigner, denying them justice. "I looked for someone among them who would build up the wall and stand before me in the gap on behalf of the land so I would not have to destroy it, but I found no one."

A gap in the wall, a gap full of guilt.
A wall with a gap will not be able to stand, it will not be able to give protection. Such walls are examples of our lives, which have been deeply injured through extortion and robbery, through oppression and illegal actions against us.

---

[42] Ezek 22:29-30

So I, Heinrich, am willing to enter the gaps of your soul caused by the sin committed against you by your earthly father. I will, as a substitute for your father, come before God and confess to you and God my sins and ask you of forgiveness.[43] As a substitute for your Father, I ask for forgiveness:

How he hurt you, what he did not give to you.

when he did not love you, did not give you his attention.

When he did not provide for you.

When he left your mother.

When he left your siblings.

When he beat you because he was drunk, threatened you, cursed you.

When he emotionally and bodily misused you and, through that, brought you into unbelievable dissension. And because all of this, ruined your childhood, made your life very hard to live.

Perhaps you were a stumbling block in his life, he didn't want a child (or no more children).

He wanted a son and you were a daughter. Or a daughter and your were a son.

He left your life when he died at an early age.

If not everything applies to your situation, then look at it as if it were not written.

We have to talk about the injuries which happened in time and space to you.

Perhaps this is the first time that someone asks you for forgiveness of these injuries and touches the painful memories. But according to what is reported in the Bible and from what Jesus said himself, forgiveness is one of the greatest weapons which exists. It can break negative bonds and set you free.

I ask you now to please stand up and imagine that I, Heinrich, have kneeled before you and as a substitute for your father, ask you to forgive me:

---

[43] Confessing sins through substitution is found many times in the Bible: Ezra, Nehemiah and Daniel in chapter 9. Also 1.Samuel 25:23-32 where Abigail asks David to forgive the sins of her husband. Romans 9, 2-3 Paul was willing to be excluded from the fellowship with Jesus for the sake of the believers. There is more written about this in our book „About Hearing", published by BOD Verlag Norderstedt.

„Dear heavenly Father, I put myself in these gaps. I bring before you, Abba, as a substitute, the guilt of this father."

And I, as a substitute for your father, plead with you, dear reader, for forgiveness
that I did not love you enough,
ignoring you, not having seen your worth,
that I gave you away, not giving you my attention,
that I did not provide all your needs,
that I left your mother,
that I left you and your siblings,
that I beated you because I was drunk, or threatened or cursed you,
that I emotionally and bodily mistreated you, which brought you into a tremendous dissention,
that I brought terrible injuries into your childhood which have made your life very difficult,
that you were a hindrance in my life because I didn't want (anymore) a child,
that you were a son and I wanted a daughter. Or you were a daughter and I wanted a son. By doing that I denied your identity, given to you by Abba,
that I abandoned you when I died at an early age.

I ask you of forgiveness for that which I, your Father, have done to you."

It would be very good if you could now forgive your father.
You can read the following suggested text out loud; the passages which do not apply to you, leave out. If you need a lot of time for this, that is OK. Just go back to this part of the book later. Perhaps you can talk with someone about this before you read it. Find someone with whom you can discuss and go through this later.

It is VERY IMPORTANT that you do not find excuses for your father.
For example: He couldn't do it any other way, he had a difficult childhood / war, his father was terrible...
YOU HAVE BEEN INJURED!
You do it for yourself, not for your father.

Suggestion:
„I forgive you now, my earthly father (it would be good to address him by name), for what you did to me.

When you did not love me, you did not encourage me, did not explain how the world works.

When you beat me, were disrespectful, threatened and misused me.

When you made me look stupid, put me down and made me ashamed.

I forgive you for not protecting me.

I forgive you for leaving our family, my mother and siblings.

I forgive you for not wanting me as your son / daughter, but wanted a daughter / son.

I forgive you for having ruined my childhood and, because of that, laying a heavy burden upon my life.

I forgive you for not wanting me.

If there are any other things which happened that we haven't mentioned here, please add them to the list now.

I bring all of this to the cross of Jesus. For all time and into eternity. I will not accuse you Papa (or add a first name) anymore.

Holy Spirit, I ask you to please come now and take the wrong memories and pain out of my heart and fill what is now empty with the peace of Abba. Amen"

I, Heinrich, was personally helped through a revelation to see why my father rejected me. He left my mother and I right after my sister was born and I was 2 years old. His rejection began in the summer of 1950. My father was obsessed with cars and always had the newest model. We, that is he, my mother and I, were sitting in a field, the car was parked next to us. My diapers were changed because I had produced waste. In those days there were no throw-away diapers, only cotton ones, which my mother had to take home with the contents. And that in his new car! Right then and there my father left my mother and I.

I was able to forgive him.

If you have been able to forgive, then I congratulate you for your big step into freedom. You have accomplished a tremendous task, even if you don't feel it in your heart or your feelings. In the spiritual world great things have happened and God your Father is very proud of you.

I have one last thing, that most fathers never do, which I want to make up for:
To bless their children. (More about this for men in chapter 8 and about women
in chapter 9) There are many examples of Blessings in the Bible, beginning with
Jacob[44] to Simeon[45] in the New Testament, who Jesus blessed.

Your father should have spoken this out over you, which I will do now:
„ I bless you with the good blessing of your ancestors. I bless you with that,
which your father had for you but wasn't able to tell you:
You are my beloved child,
I wanted you
and I am so happy to have you.
That, which God your Father laid within you, I bring to life with this blessing. So
that your abilities and gifts may blossom and been seen. Amen"

Martina McBride sang a song that expresses exactly these thoughts:
„My baby loves me just the way that I am."
One only has to substitute the word Daddy or Abba for Baby. (Text to song is in
the attachment)

---

[44] Genesis 49
[45] Luke 2, 25 ff

Jesus tells about his father.

In order to know God the Father more closely, we would need to ask someone who has seen him face to face and can tell us about him because we cannot SEE him.[46] But there is someone, only one, who saw him and knows him: Jesus Christ, his son.

Jesus said[47] „All things have been delivered unto me of my Father: and no one knoweth the Son, save the Father; neither doth any know the Father, save the Son, and he to whomsoever the Son willeth to reveal [him.]"

John writes:[48] „No one has ever seen God; the only Son, who is in the bosom of the Father, he has made him known."

In the book of Hebrews:[49]"The Son is the radiance of God's glory and the exact representation of his being,".

Paul wrote in the letter to the Colossians:[50] „For in Christ all the fullness of the Deity lives in bodily form,".

We have a wonderful story which Luke passed on to us[51]. Jesus describes his Father in a very touching and surprising way: The Parable of the lost Son; it should be named of the two lost sons, even better the Parable of God the Father.

Before Luke wrote this parable about the lost son, he wrote two other parables about Loosing, Seeking and Finding:

The parable of the lost sheep.

The Good Shepherd leaves his 99 sheep alone in order to go and find the one lost sheep. When he finds it, it isn't a romantic story, as we often see in pictures: the lost sheep is happy to see the shepherd and let's him gladly carry him back home on his shoulders.

No, in reality, the sheep panics because he doesn't recognize the shepherd, as

---

[46] Exodus 33, 20
[47] Matt 11, 27, similar in Luke 10,22 and John 14,6
[48] John 1, 18
[49] Heb. 1, 3a
[50] Col. 2, 9
[51] Luke 15, 11-32

we were once told during a conversation with a shepherd. The sheep fights against being rescued with all its might! The shepherd has to throw the sheep on its back so he can tie its legs together, places it on his shoulders, speaks encouragingly to it and carries it, until it has calmed down. And then he calls all of his friends and neighbors so they can share his joy and celebrate that he found his lost sheep.

We are so important to God our Father, even though the story is about a herd of sheep. One out of a hundred is so valuable for him!

The next parable is about the lost coin.

A housewife misses a certain coin and looks everywhere in her house, sweeps and turns everything over to try to find the coin. Finally she finds the missing coin and invites her neighbors over to celebrate with her, as in the first parable. That is how important we are to God our Father, even though this parable has to do with objects. One out of ten is very precious to him.

At the end of every parable is told how all celebrate over having found what was lost. Yes, the reign of joy is spoken about. The joy of finding that which had been lost.

Let's go back to the Parable about the two sons. Whenever the Bible speaks of sons,

daughters are also always meant. In Job the daughters are named by name; we are not told the names of the sons.

Verse 11
Jesus continued: „A man had two sons."
Then Jesus continued to speak. He told the 3 parables one after the other; the three of them build one story.

A man had 2 sons. As we interpret the text, there was nothing which gives the impression that they were rich. It is interesting to see that Jesus spoke of the man as having had two sons, which could mean that he lost both of them. Both of them did not identify, did not feel or accept themselves as being a son. In the following text, when speaking about the son, the daughters are also referred to.

Verse 12

The younger one said to him, "Father, give me my share of the property now.'
So the man divided his property between his two sons.

The younger son, the second-born, saw no chance for himself since his older brother was in charge of the work at home. The younger one thought „He will inherit everything and I will get nothing." That is the way the younger son viewed the facts. However, facts and our view of them do not express the truth of God the Father. Looking upon the facts in our own lives takes our eyes away from the truth. A good example of this is the bumble bee. According to aerodynamic laws, she should not be able to fly: The surface of her wings are too small. The bumble bee doesn't know this, so she flies! Why? Because God the Father created her and gave her this ability. The best example in the Old Testament is Sarah.[52] The fact was that Sarah was 90 (ninety!) years old,[53] Abraham was 100, which made it impossible to have children! But Sarah bore Isaac. That was the truth of God the Father.

Sometimes facts can mislead us to do things which we had better not done. As Sarah did when she was unwilling to wait any longer for the fulfillment of the promise to have a son. She took the matter into her own hands by giving her maiden Hagar to Abraham as his second wife.[54] Ishmael, the oldest son, was the father of a tremendous folk, who are the ancestors of the middle east conflicts between Israel and the surrounding countries.

Back to the younger son: He turned away from his father because of the facts of the situation as he saw it. Away from the borrowed identity of being his father's son. He went so far as to declare that, for him,
his father was dead. For he could not demand his inheritance before the testator has died. His relationship to his father means nothing more to him. He sees it as slavery, which he wants to flee from. He wants to separate himself from his father. It wasn't the father who threw him out of the house, after the unbelievable demand from his son to give him his inheritance. That would have been understandable!
Jesus explains in very clear words what sin is according to the Bible. In the

---

[52] Gen 17 + 18 + 21
[53] Gen 17,17
[54] Gen 16

German word „Suende", which means sin, we can find two other words which help to describe what sin is and how it effects us. The first word we find is the word Strait. The Fehmarnsund , over which a bridge is built, is in the Ostsee (East Sea) and divides the island Fehmarn from the continent. Strait means division, a trench, a gap. The other word which helps to define sin is shame. I am ashamed for what I have done, I hide myself, I intensify the separation. The best example of this is Adam and Eve, after having eaten from the apple[55]. They discovered that they were naked, stood naked before God and wove fig leaves together, as quickly as possible, and covered themselves. They were ashamed. The absolute trust of a child in its father was gone! They realized that they had been completely open with their father up until now, but they had destroyed that trust.

The son wants to separate himself from his father: I want to be separated from my father, I will do what I want to do. I want to be in charge of myself. Just as the serpent promised Adam and Eve: You will be like God. I don't want anyone to tell me what to do, no one take care of me, I know myself what is good for me. I know what is good for me, what I like. I am I.

The son mistrusted the Father which destroyed his part of the relationship. Sin is separation from God. It is a **broken relationship and not something bad we have done.** Mistrust is the beginning of all separation from God.

But the father divides his possessions among his two sons. Among both! The Greek word here is ousia = belongings, money, property, everything which the father owned. Both receive that which the father had planned to give them. He gave them everything.

There are no bad words to be heard from the father, no litigation is aimed for, no words like „that won't work", no „what are you doing to me" is spoken by the father. Certainly the father feels sadness in his heart about his son leaving. Perhaps he tried again to reach his son's heart and enjoy some last happy days together.

By the way, there was no word about having lost half of the wealth!

---

[55] Gen 3, 7

Here are some notes from the Talmud.[56]

The authors warn about dividing up inheritance while the testator is still alive. If that had to be done, then only by obeying the rule that the inheritor was not allowed to sell the property as long as the testator was still alive. That meant that the Father had to willingly give over his inheritance, as well as his agreement, to sell the land.

And then there was another rule in the Talmud that the oldest child would get 2/3 and the second child only 1/3. That could also have been reason enough to feel at a disadvantage.

And this situation was a shame for the family in the village, in which, as very differently today in big cities, the whole village found out about it in a short time. More about that later.

Verse 13

After a few days the younger son sold his part of the inheritance and left home with the money. He went to a country far away, where he wasted his money in reckless living.

The son was absolutely determined to find his happiness as he wished. What he had been given by his father meant nothing to him, so he sold it. That which had belonged to his father, was now owned by strangers. And they exploited all of it. What have I sold to get away from God? In order to achieve what I wanted to? We once heard in a sermon that every idol requires a sacrifice. What have I already sacrificed?

And the son, unknown by all those he meets and passes, continues his journey. The distant country must have been overseas, perhaps in Spain or Morocco, after what people understood about the world at that time. As far away from home as possible, from his father. Now he can finally do what he had always wanted to do. Create a new identity for himself. Fit for fun, as is said today. Of course he finds new friends, but they were more interested in his possessions than in him.

---

[56]Talmud: the Talmud (Hebrewתַּלְמוּד Teachings, Studies,) is one of the most important scripts of the Jews. It is made up of two parts, the older Mischna and the younger Gemara, and consists of two editions, the *Babylonian* and the *Jerusalem Talmud*. It doesn't include any biblical Texts of the Law (Torah), but explains how these rules in the official use and in everyday life of the Rabbis were understood and explained.

He led a lavish life, as we can read in other translations. No thoughts were wasted on the future, no thoughts that the money would someday run out.
In German we have a saying which says: „People are punished the worst when they are allowed to have things go their way."
What generations had built up over years did not tolerate the son's chosen lavish way of life. There was no increase in anything; what was there, ran very quickly through his fingers. Easy come, easy go.

Verse 14
He spent everything he had. Then a severe famine spread over that country, and he was left without a thing.
After he had used up everything he had, unexpected difficulties arose. A famine! Jesus explained the difficulties very aptly. Today we are well informed about famines. One only has to click from one television program to the other. The hunger for recognition. I'm somebody, too! Don't you all see that? What do I have to do to finally be noticed by others? How much more do I have to twist the reality of who I am so others will accept me? How much would it cost to at least be noticed for a short length of time? A rampage or terror attack, which happens more and more.
Our self-made identity does not help us through such difficulties.

Verse 15
So he went to work for one of the citizens of that country, who sent him out to his farm to take care of the pigs.
All of his new friends had left him. There is nothing left for them to take. The recognition is gone! Who is interested in a poor beggar? His identity, that was built upon his money, is gone. He turned to one of the citizens of that country, someone who owned civil rights, which was very unusual at that time. Paul was very aware of the privileges of his Roman civil rights and made use of them![57]
But this son did not own these rights, he didn't even buy them. Forgot to buy them.
The only thing he could sell was himself; I almost wanted to write prostitution, as we will see later. Und this has become very common today.
The younger son does **not** manage the farm **anymore** but has become a slave =

---

[57] Acts 16, 37 + 38; Acts 22, 25 – 29; Acts 25,11

one who has to obey commands given by others. The only thing left for him to do was to look for a job: sheparding pigs. But pigs are regarded by the Jews as unclean animals, which one was to avoid being near. Now he didn't only have to do with that which was unclean, but he also had to care for it, which was unheard of by those who heard Jesus tell this parable. That is how far a person can really fall.

Verse 16
He wished he could fill himself with the bean pods the pigs ate, but no one gave him anything to eat.
The situation gets worse: he is not even allowed to eat what the unclean animals are given. It is hard to imagine such a situation! Just think about it – he had to watch the pigs eat the bean pods he gave them and his stomach was grumbling. He did not trust himself to take any of this feed for the pigs out of fear of losing his job. That was the only thing left that he had.
No one wanted to give him anything. But why should they? Slaves had no rights, his master could sell him or kill him.
Having enough food at home had never been a problem. He began to remember that...

Verse 17
At last he came to his senses and said, "All my father's hired workers have more than they can eat, and here I am about to starve!"
Now he had reached a real crisis in his life. He turned his thoughts inward and found the courage to face what was going on inside of him.
The Chinese language, which doesn't have any letters but only pictures or signs, writes the word „crisis" with two signs written next to each other: a sign for danger and a sign for chance. Both signs describe beautifully the word crisis: danger and chance at the same time.
It was easy to see the danger. He would soon starve where he was if something didn't change. He saw his chance after taking inventory of his situation: „Here I will die but those who work daily for my father have enough to eat." It doesn't occur to him though to think about his guilt or how he treated his father nor to join in the complaint as found in a Psalm:[58] „Bring us back, O God!"

---

[58] Psalm 80

At least he changes the direction in which he is looking. For the first time he does not look away from his Father's house but looks towards it! Now it is a comparison of how things are where he is and how they were at home. Even though he had claimed his father to be dead, he still had at least a memory, a good memory of him. That is something that is deeply anchored in each one of us, a memory of a Father House, a quiet, protected place. Or at least a life-long yearning for that, an imagination of how it could have been.

Verse 18
„I will get up and go to my father and say, "Father, I have sinned against God and against you."
After taking inventory of his situation he makes a decision, a wonderful decision. With deep assurance he decides not to continue living the way he had been doing, but to reverse his direction, to turn around. This process of reversing one's direction can be understood as the biblical meaning for repentance. This has nothing to do with sitting out a term of punishment. But, reversing ones direction means to look in another direction, to change ones thoughts about something. One could take a chance and say: He made a decision to follow Jesus, because Jesus said: „I am the Way, I am the Truth and I am the Life. No one comes to the Father except though me."[59] How else could he have found his way back?
Nevertheless he wants to be a slave again. He thought: I still have my rights. I will work as a day laborer. However, he didn't even have the right to be a slave for they also had their rights. His rights did not exist anymore since he had declared them to be dead.
But he hadn't yet found the words to say to excuse himself for what he had done. He thinks up a statement, a confession of what he had done wrong: separating himself from Heaven and his Father. At least he does realize that he had not only disrespected his Father (4. commandment)[60] but had also separated himself from God. There isn't much longing of repentance in him; he just wants to get out of this present situation.

Verse 19

---

[59] John 14,6
[60] Exodus 20,12

„I am no longer worthy to be called your son; make me like one of your hired servants."

I am not worthy. That is quite a serious statement coming from the younger son. He lost his advantages and position of being the younger son, he knows that; however he hopes he will be successful in some other way. Maybe because he remembers that his father found all people worthy. That is what he wants to achieve, not to be freed from guilt, but to find a place to stay, work as a day laborer. That would be enough. The main thing is to get out of the situation he is in.

Still wanting to have something from his father, although he had declared him as dead. Although he left him. He'd had no second thoughts about his father when he had left him. But now his father is back in his thoughts.

Verse 20

So he got up and went to his father. But while he was still a long way off, his father saw him and was filled with compassion for him; he ran to his son, threw his arms around him and kissed him.

He probably imagined what the situation would be like when he stands before his father. He knew he did not have any more rights. For his inheritance had already been paid out to him. He knew he was coming to his father as a beggar, dependent upon his voluntary help. For that reason he formulated his sentences with the demand to be hired as a Tucker, a Servant or a Slave.

Let's take a look at the father. How did he get along while his son was gone? "But while he was still a long way off, his father saw him," is written above. Hildegard and I often go on vacation in South France. She loves to lie out on the beach, that is not what I enjoy. So we decide at which time I will meet her there, then we swim together or go for a walk. Around the time I am supposed to arrive, she begins to look to see if I am almost there. There he is, no, it wasn't him. When she is sure it is me, she jumps up and runs to greet me. Of course she knows at which approximate time I will arrive.

That is how God our Father is! He doesn't look only at the agreed time, but **always.**

He looks after his children every day, especially after those who are far away. He cries his eyes out for them. He hopes they will come. He searches very closely with his eyes for those who are far away from him and who have said that he is dead. He is the one who suffers under the separation. He still loves his children. His love to us makes him very vulnerable. Who wants a God who cries, looks for those who are lost, to whom his love for his children has highest priority? Who leaves the 99 sheep alone in order to look for the one lost sheep? Who looks through the whole house just to find one coin, although he already has nine others.

We love the picture of the Prodigal son painted by Rembrandt. While on a business trip, I, Heinrich, had the great honor to be able to look at this very big painting in St. Petersburg in the Hermitage. What touched me the most were the Father's eyes.

They are not fixed upon the son standing before him! As if they were saying:"Now he is here with me, but where are the other children for whom I cry my eyes out? Day and night I look for them!" And I had the impression that his eyes wandered through the room to search for his children and to look where they were. It touched my heart and moved me so deeply that tears rushed into my eyes, as I stood there among all the other visitors of the museum.

It is similar to the Parable about the 10 coins: He, the Father, prepared everything for the return of his son, the house had been swept clean. Just by doing that wasn't enough to get his son back. Everything has been prepared for the return of all of his children, whom he looks for day and night.

Or like the Parable about the 99 sheep. We went on vacation with our trailer in the South of France and had parked near a sheep farm. Rain came up and the shepherd led all the sheep back into the stall. It wasn't possible though to get all the lambs and their mothers into the stall before it started to rain, so some of them got wet. All of a sudden there were so many sheep calling! We asked the shepherd why they all called so loud? He said: because of the rain their smell had changed and the lambs couldn't find their mother any more.

That is what happens with us and our Father. The world has changed the „scent" of our Father and we can't find him anymore.

In the parable the father saw his son coming and was deeply touched. But that doesn't exactly describe how he felt inside: His guts were making strange sounds, his innermost being was in turmoil. His emotions were overwhelming. He wasn't in control of himself any more. Perhaps because he saw what was going on inside of his son. Just as Jesus was able to see in the Samarian woman at Jacob'swell.[61] He ran to his son!

To be more exact, he runs towards us.

The father did not stand angrily waiting for his son to come throw himself down on the ground before him to ask of forgiveness. This is a picture we often have of God, but he is not angry with us! He is angry about the sin which has bound us so that we cannot find him. But he is not angry at us. He loves us.

Not only that, he runs towards us!!

He runs towards his son!

The son did not run faster when he saw his father. The Father recognized him, saw he was coming home and immediately jumped up to run to him.

As soon as we give up our shame, God will come very quickly to us. He runs!

That was absolutely unheard of for those listening to Jesus at that time. An older person never ran towards a younger one! Never did a person of a higher position run to one of a lower. Never did the Father run to his son. It is always just the opposite. Yes, it is because of God's mercy that he let that happen. And that is not all!

In order for the Father to run, he had to pull up his coat and his leg coverings or else he would trip over them. And it is Taboo in the Orient, a No No, to show ones naked legs in public.

But that didn't bother the father one bit! What are Taboos worth when he had the chance to have his son again!

God comes to us!

---

[61] John 4, 16-18

That is the central statement of this parable. God comes to us and doesn't wait until we throw ourselves on the ground before his throne. He comes to him who declared him as dead, who sold and wasted everything which he'd been given. He comes to those who have wasted their lives and their inheritance. He loves the sinner, the lost and those who are separated from him. I can come to God the Father **with** my problems, **with** my guilt, **with** my shame, **with** my anger.

What a difference to how the people of Israel met God in the Sinai desert.[62] Thunder and Lightning! In verse 17 we read that Moses leads his people to meet God. But in our parable, God ran toward his son, not toward a tremendous group of people.

God became weak and vulnerable out of love for sinners. Love makes God the Father assailable. Love makes the Father weak, at least in our eyes. **That** is the way he is, says Jesus to us. His love for his son did not stand in the way of his love for sinners. And he even gave his son for us. So that he is not separated from sinners anymore.

Another remark about the Talmud:
There was a ceremony to prohibit the „lost" son from coming back, who had caused so much shame. The whole village had to stand together to keep him from coming back, to
chase him out of the village. That is what the Father in all cases wanted to hinder when he saw him and ran to him. To keep that from happening.

The parable gets even better.
The Father threw his arms around his son's neck and hugged him . He almost ran over him. And he kisses him. A kiss is a sign of love, even between men![63] Also between bride and groom, parents and their children, siblings and other relatives. A kiss is a sign of reconciliation.[64]
In another translation we can read: „He kissed him to the ground." Actually he deserved a whipping, but a kiss?

---

[62] Exo 19, 7-25
[63] Exo 4,27; 2. Sam 20,9
[64] Gen 33, 4:45, 15; 2, Sam 20, 9

That was the Father's Greeting. **Before** the son had a chance to say anything. The happiness that he had his son again, overwhelmed him. He is interested in his son and not how he failed. He saw his son, as God the Father had always seen him.

If we have children and one of them comes running home, crying, from the playground because it hurt itself, we do not think first about whether we will get dirty when we hug our child. Our Father in Heaven is just the same.

In the book „The Shack"[65] this event is beautifully explained to the protagonist Mack. He nears the shack, the door is suddenly opened and a fat Afro-American lady (the author Paul Young has a woman play the role of God, in order to change our perception of God) pulls the surprised Mack to herself, lifts him up high and hugs him. Before he can say a word.

Verse 21
"The son said to him, 'Father, I have sinned against heaven and against you. I am no longer worthy to be called your son.'
How does the son greet his father? Other translations use the word „but". But his son spoke. Here the word „but" expresses surprise. He didn't plan to say what he said. The first word he spoke was „Father", which stands in contrast to the last words in his formulated sentence. There he said he wasn't worthy to be called his son anymore. He was very surprised over the words he spoke and is then able to make his confession of guilt to his Father, which he had formulated while on his way home.

In the sentence „ **I am no longer worthy to be called your son.**" he is expressing the thought that his father is not rich enough, not generous enough nor good enough to let him become his son again. However this confession of his sin is different from the prefabricated version he had planned on his way home.
The demand: „Let me be a day-laborer for you!" is missing!
Perhaps because his father's greeting was such an expression of love, the son was overcome by his own guilt towards his father. Or he had learned from Jesus on the way back to his father's house that his own father had no slaves. Or what he had first planned to say didn't go along with addressing his father by name. We are first of all our Father's children. No matter what we have done. Please

---

[65] The Shack by William Paul Young, Windblown Media Inc.

61

do not misunderstand what I am saying; I don't mean that we should misuse the love and trust of our father by doing a lot of wrong things. Paul and others warn us against that.[66] Just as we remain the children of our parents, no matter what we have done wrong, we remain the children of God the Father who wanted us and loves us unconditionally.

What else we see here: The son didn't offer to work as long as needed in order to pay off his wrongs. He would never be able to do that. That was impossible!

And now he waits to see how his Father reacts.
A thunderstorm, a flood of accusations, the pain of waiting for this moment for all those years, the tears...

Verse 22
"But the father said to his servants, 'Quick! Bring the best robe and put it on him. Put a ring on his finger and sandals on his feet."
„**BUT** the Father" is written here. The word „But" wipes out all that was said before. His father surprisingly doesn't mention his son's confession of guilt. He didn't even say: I forgive you. No accusations, nothing like that! He accepts his son FULLY, just as he is.
BUT, he doesn't quit there! At the beginning of the younger son's contemplations of what he would say to his father, he'd decided to ask to be a day-laborer in order to make up for all he had wasted. And now his Father says **to** his daily workers: Take away what my son has on and quickly bring the best robes for him. Nothing is said about him taking a shower. His son is immediately given back his identity! The daily workers put the new clothes on him; he probably isn't sure how to deal with such beautiful clothes. The only thing which is now important for him to do, or to let be done to him, is his rehabilitation. Almost all that is under the new clothes is old. Here a parallel from Paul[67] „Therefore, if anyone is in Christ, the new creation has come: The old has gone, the new is here!" The old guy is still under the new clothes! And this is how the return to our Father begins for each of us.

---

[66] Rom 6,15; Hebrew 10,26
[67] 2. Cor. 5,17 and Eph 4, 22 -24

And then the ring. It is a signet-ring. The younger son is now allowed to close contracts in his father's name. The new old son is given legal power. And he has a new job: not looking out for pigs for a citizen of the country where he had been, but is given the Power of Attorney for his Father.

And then the shoes. The slaves and day-laborers at that time didn't wear any shoes. Those were only worn by people of a higher class. The son is not a day laborer anymore.

Because of our work we have been to Black Africa, south of the Sahara Desert. Still today the day-laborers and slaves do not wear shoes. Perhaps they can afford to buy themselves flip-flops, but not shoes.

The son has been placed back into his former identity. Similar to what Paul wrote in Colossians:[68] „Once you were alienated from God and were enemies in your minds because of your evil behavior. But now he has reconciled you by Christ's physical body through death."

That is God our Father. He restores and doesn't only forgive. What we have lost, he gives back to us. Abba God is the only one who can do that.[69] And wants to. Because he loves his children.

Jesus emphasizes very clearly that all is dependent upon our Father. We must keep our eyes upon him and not upon our failings of the past or our present guilt. Many Christians go through life with this suspicion: „It isn't enough." What a BIG lie!
For everything is dependent upon the Father, not upon us.

Verse 23
„Bring the fattened calf and kill it. Let's have a feast and celebrate."

His Father doesn't leave it at that! He has planned a big celebration! The

---

[68] Col 1,21b-22a
[69] Joel 2, 25

fattened calf is going to be slaughtered! The young son's return is going to be celebrated with a big feast. Let us be happy and do not look back at that which we have lost, at the past, at that which was wrong. Our Father is always future-oriented, no thoughts about the very difficult past. It is a feast because his son, whom he thought was dead, has returned. That is very miraculous.

Verse 24
„For this son of mine was dead and is alive again; he was lost and is found.' So they began to celebrate."
„My son was dead." He had lost his relationship to his father and had lost his identity. It is just like removing a embryo from the mother's womb. It dies. When our relationship to God our Father is lost, our inner man dies. Perhaps we could even say, we lose our identity. But that can come back to life. It can become full of life again. Through the relationship and nearness to our Father. Several years ago the Bible verse of the year was[70] „ But as for me, it is good to be near God. I have made the Sovereign Lord my refuge; I will tell of all your deeds. " Just to be near you is complete happiness for me. That is what the younger son learned when he was so far away from home. Through almost starving. Quite appropriate.
His father speaks to him again as „my son". His identity, his relationship to his father has been restored. Everyone needs to be spoken to by God as „You are my daughter", „You are my son".
Even Jesus needed this assurance from his Father. When he was baptized God spoke to him:[71] „You are my beloved Son!" Not until Jesus' bonding to his Father had been spoken out, was he able to begin his ministry. And we can't begin fulfilling our „Calling" until we know we are his child. Then we have the unfaltering assurance that we are the beloved children of our Father.
And they were all filled with great joy after all the years of waiting and looking to see if he
would return home.

What is the difference in the younger son's situation at the beginning of the Parable and now?

_____

[70] Motto of the Moravian Church for 2014 taken of Psalm 73, 28
[71] Matth 3,17

The son had everything before he left home; but, however, now he knows that he is loved.

The Happy End of the Parable for the younger son. Even though he didn't say anything after his confession of guilt, he is completely overwhelmed with his Father's reaction.

That is our prayer for you, dear reader, that the revelation of the Father will completely change your life.

There is a parallel story in the Old Testament in which something similar, to that which happened at the beginning of this Parable, also happened.[72] Jacob, who had deceived his brother Esau several times, came back to Canaan and had a very bad conscience because of having deceived and tricked his brother in very many ways. It is wonderful to read how he tries to get Esau to be merciful with him and brings him gifts. And then how Esau reacts!

We found a story in a magazine which was told as if it had happened at this day and time. The story has parallels with the story of the prodigal son and enables one to feel a touch of love.

A man was travelling home with the train. On his journey he told the other passengers his story.

He had lived in luxury, he lied, deceived, stole...His cheated his parents with whom he lived and treated them as if they were dirt. He had set his sights very high, felt like he was capable of more than what he'd done until now, and the poor, meager life of his parents was repugnant to him, which had the consequence that he ended up in prison.

There he realized what he had done, and most of all, what he had done to his parents. He was very ashamed, was very sorry for what he had done. And he wished so much to be able to go back home.

Shortly before he was released from prison, he wrote his parents a letter with the request that they hang a white flag in a tree, which he should be able to see from the train. The flag would be a symbol that his parents wanted him to come home. If he saw the flag he would get out of the train; otherwise he would just continue his journey.

He was so excited, that he asked a fellow passenger to look to see if he saw a

---

[72] Gen 32 and 33

tree with a white flag. The passenger suddenly yelled out "The tree is full of white flags hanging from the branches!"

Now we will look at the second part of the Parable which has a very different character:

Verse 25

The older son was out in the field. When he came home, he heard from afar all the noise of music and dancing.

Let us take a look at the older son. He did not look to see when his brother would come home, as his father had done. He wouldn't have noticed him anyway, because the first-born were always working. Not without reason did he stay at home. There had to be someone who would do the work when his younger brother was gone. He had to be sure that everything kept going. He was responsible for the farm.

But the word „responsibility", as meant here, is not written in the Bible! In the Elberfelder translation of the Old Testament that word is not found at all! In the NGÜ (New Geneva Translation) of the New Testament the word is found five times, but means here having to give account of something. And it is very biblical, especially when Jesus talks about the Parable of the Overseer.[73] Giving account of what we have done. This parable comes right after the Parable we are talking about, as Jesus is trying to draw our attention to it.

It is never used to mean to carry responsibility. That produces pressure on the reader or listener. From others or from myself. How many burdens have we laid upon ourselves and others have laid upon us? Responsibility has nothing to do with being a child. Young children do not carry responsibility, even our judicial system knows that.

The older son would never take the chance of declaring his father as dead. Did he really know who his father was? Did he know how he father suffered? He didn't even notice that his father had kept Watch day and night, to see when his son would return home. He lives next to him but knows little or nothing about his father's mourning. He acted more like an employee. Employees can protest and be dissatisfied, complain about low wages, go on strike, and give notice. If my boss doesn't give me a pay raise, then I have lost all interest in him. He is not

---

[73] Luke 16, 1 -8

treating me fairly. He doesn't see that all that belongs to his father, belongs to him also.

The older son found his worth and identity in what he did, not from who he was. Music and dancing were disturbing! Perhaps he got upset because a celebration was going on. And when one can't do anything anymore, one is worthless.

That means he had to do more. For his Father. For God. For Jesus. But God our Father doesn't employ children, doesn't support child labor!
Is what I am doing my commission from God? Or did I decide by myself to do this to earn God's love? The younger son, as we saw in the beginning of the Parable, was not interested in doing anything for his father. And ended up ruining his life. The older son is not any different. He decided himself what he was going to do. And what happens if my plans do not work out?
When I, Heinrich, began my career in the 1970s, I began working in the IT department of a big company. There was a man in this department in his mid-fifties, who sat alone in a corner and worked with the computer system. He had no contact with the other employees in this department. I asked him what he did and he said he was maintaining a system that wasn't being used anymore! Several years before he had been in charge of the data system hall. 30 young women sat in the hall and made invoices of the bills of the company on punch cards. He was very proud to be in charge of this department and to be able to correct anything the women did wrong. I was told that he walked through the rows of workers with a proud look and his chest held very upright. Very aware of his power. During the development of the IT branch the data processing hall was not needed anymore. The acquisition of data wandered back to where it had begun. His life's work was meaningless. He wasn't needed anymore. From one moment to the next.

We did not find any examples of people in the Bible who were given a certain responsibility to carry out. Commissions are given, in the Old and New Testaments. And with commissions the „employer" carries the responsibility and the employee is held accountable for what he has done. That is right. But when something doesn't work out, then he is not responsible for it. We just can't do that! Neither for ourselves nor for others. We have tasks as marriage partners, as parents to our children, in the church and in our Bible Study Groups.

But the responsibility is carried by God the Father. Because he is the only one who can make something good out of our mistakes. If that weren't the case, we would fall into doubt. God our Father can do that.
More about this in the chapter **About Responsibility.**

Here is just a short but important detail: The older son **heard from afar** the noise of the music and dancing, the father **saw** his younger son from afar. The results are completely different, the older son is enraged, the Father is filled with Love. Listening is important but seeing is even more important.

Verse 26
„So he called one of the servants and asked him what was going on."
The older son did not react as his father. He did not go himself to find out what was going on. That is surprising. He sent a slave to find out what had happened. We see he was surprised and perhaps somewhat angered about the celebration. He let someone tell him what had happened instead of himself going to see. Listening what someone else said was more important to him than hearing an answer himself. Secondhand information, instead of experiencing it himself.

Verse 27
„'Your brother has come,' he replied, 'and your father has killed the fattened calf because he has him back safe and sound.'
Your brother has come home. The older brother had never thought about how his brother might be doing. His enragement over his younger brother loosing half of the inheritance occupied his mind. For him, his brother was dead. Banished from his heart. This story reminds us of what happened between Cain and Abel[74], in which the events led up to the critical question: „ Then the Lord said to Cain, "Where is your brother Abel?" "I don't know," he replied. **"Am I my brother's keeper?"**
The Father was so happy that his younger son had returned, he let the fattened calf be slaughtered. In Germany a fattened calf is usually slaughtered when it is 22 weeks old. If one waits longer, it is not a calf anymore but a young cow. That is a very short time in comparison to the length of time the younger son was gone. To say it in a different way, during the absence of the younger son there

---

[74] Gen 4

were many religious holidays when fattened calves had been slaughtered. Surely the older son ate the very special meal. But not now, when his brother returned. This day is a celebration only for the father because his son came back doing well, except for the rags he wore and how much weight he had lost.

Verse 28
„The older brother became angry and refused to go in. So his father went out and pleaded with him.“
The older son got very angry, probably because of the fattened calf. How can his father slaughter it on a day that is not a religious holiday? But how valuable is a fattened calf compared to his brother? And the older son is offended. He doesn't go in the house. Doesn't want to take part in the celebration. Wants to pamper his anger and his disappointment. He was the one who excluded himself, not the Father nor the brother. And then came what was so astonishing: his father also comes to him, he **leaves** the celebration to talk with his older son. Here we see the obliging, kind father. God our Father does not only come to those who have turned away from him; no, also to those who live with him. Or at least near him. Or who labored hard for him, as we will see.
His father speaks kindly to him. Luther translated: „He begs him!!“ God the Father asks him and asks you to come in. We are invited to celebrate with him! There are no accusations: Why didn't you greet your brother, why are you ruining the celebration, why do you have a problem with my happiness?

Verse 29
„But he answered his father, 'Look! All these years I've been slaving for you and never disobeyed your orders. Yet you never gave me even a young goat so I could celebrate with my friends.“
That was the straw that broke the camel's back! He accuses his Father: „You, Father, do not handle things right! I have been serving you for so many years!“ But God our Father doesn't want any servants. He has them already, the angels serve him day and night. He wants to have children and Jesus speaks about this time and again.
Now to the story of Martha and Maria as written in Luke:[75] „But Martha was distracted by all the preparations that had to be made. She came to him and

---

[75] Luke 10, 40 - 42

asked, "Lord, don't you care that my sister has left me to do the work by myself? Tell her to help me!"

"Martha, Martha," the Lord answered, "you are worried and upset about many things, but few things are needed—or indeed only one. Mary has chosen what is better, and it will not be taken away from her." That is what it is all about: To be near the Father and not think I have to earn being able to be close to him. This can be dangerous for all those never-ending helpers in churches and fellowships. Then someone comes who is accepted into the church as a prodigal son. While the others work, organize and labor. For years. And they lose their childhood with God the father.

„I have never disobeyed your requests." In other translations we read: ...and have never disobeyed your precepts (Luther). I have done everything that you told me to do. ("Hoffnung für alle", a German translation).

Not even the scribes allowed themselves to say such words. When they heard Jesus' demand:[76] „Who ever is without sin can throw the first stone.", they left the scene.

But the older son is determined to be in the right. That is also a sickness of the Germans. If we are asked if we would rather be right or happy, 2/3 answer: To be right. And that is the situation the older son is in. Rather be right than be happy and celebrate with the others.

„You never gave me even a young goat so I could celebrate with my friends." A young goat costs around 3 – 4 Dollars. It sounds like the older son had nothing to say on his father's farm. But that wasn't the case, as we can see in Verse 26. He was in a position to tell his servants what to do. But then, he didn't even think to ask his father for a young goat! Instead he expected that his hard work would be seen and rewarded. Although everything belonged to him, as we can read in Verse 12!

I sometimes have the impression that God the Father stands by and watches how we work our heads off for the church and fellowships and thinks: Why do they do this out of their own strength? Why do they not ask: Is his my task? Or: What is my task? Why do they not bring my children to me and lay them in my lap instead of making them be servants and overload them with responsibilities,

---

[76] John 8,7

which they cannot carry?

The older son is filled with deep mistrust for his father:"My father doesn't see me, doesn't reward me." Mistrust always leads away from God the Father. Mistrust is the beginning of separation, which is begun from our side.

It is interesting that the older son doesn't address his father by his name Father, but begins immediately throwing accusations at him. He is very angry! Just the opposite of how the younger brother addressed his father; he began with a salutation and confessing his guilt to his Father.

Verse 30
„But when this son of yours who has squandered your property with prostitutes comes home, you kill the fattened calf for him!"
„This son of yours" (not my brother), sounded very disrespectful, as if he was trying to say he didn't want to have anything to do with him.
He squandered all of your wealth with prostitutes. „Your wealth", it was divided up among both sons, as we can read in Verse 12. The older son had not yet accepted his part of the inheritance. And how does he know that his younger brother had squandered his part of the inheritance with prostitutes? It was not written down anywhere and his younger brother would not have told him that! What does that have to say about the older brother? We accuse others of things which are not true: perhaps because we would have liked to do them, but were too much of a coward. Or we didn't ask our father because we were afraid to. Or, although we always wanted to do that, we never did because of fear of God our Father. But Jesus had this to say:[77]"But I tell you that anyone who looks at a woman lustfully has already committed adultery with her in his heart."

He would not have been surprised, had his brother done that, because he thought he was willing to do anything of the sort. But he did not think that he would come home. And then there was the envy about the fattened calf. But he did not know about the ring, the new clothes and the shoes.
That it going to be a big shock for him!
Let's look at the Father again. He loves those who make problems for us. He

---

[77] Matt 5,28

supports and helps those who we reject. And what is the worth of the younger son who is dressed in rags and has nothing left? And about whom I can get very angry!

In order to overcome such selfish and egoistic attitudes, I, Heinrich, ask God the Father this question: Show me what about this person makes you want to love him. The answers God the Father has given me have made me quite ashamed of my hard-heartedness.

Verse 31
" 'My son,' the father said, 'you are always with me, and everything I have is yours."

His father speaks very lovingly to him although he is confronted by his son's accusations and had wished to hear and see a different reaction. My child, to be more exact - my little child. That is who the oldest son is for the father. His child. Even if his son yells his anger and accusations in his father's face, he is still his son. We remain children of God, even when we, while sitting on his lap, beat him on his chest. He is willing to take that.

You are always with me! You are always near me, even when you do not feel this. You will always be in my heart – even when you do not allow me to be part of your life anymore. Come back.
Jesus said: [78] "Let the little children come to me, and do not hinder them, for the kingdom of heaven belongs to such as these." We interpret this verse so: Let the little child in you come to me, to the Father. The adult part of you should not keep you from coming to me, your Father. Perhaps because of misunderstandings or other reasons. We will talk about this in the next chapter. Being a child, **that** is the Identity of both sons, but the older son rejects this. His father sees his wounded heart. For a moment he sees only his older son and does not think about his younger son having just come home and the celebration for him. He briefly forgets his other child as the shepherd forgot the

---

[78] Matt 19,14

99 sheep.

And then we read about the contrasting words „You are always with me" and „All these years I've been slaving for you." The first statement describes a permanent situation, the second reckons with all the terrible years. The Father, who sees the abyss of hatred against the younger brother, is hurt very deeply .

Everything that belongs to me, belongs to you also.

A basic statement about the relationship of God the Father to Jesus. Luke writes:[79]

 "All things have been committed to me by my Father."

Jesus said: **All things have been committed to me by my Father.** John writes:[80] **„The Father loves the Son and has placed everything in his hands."** and **„Jesus gave them this answer: "Very truly I tell you, the Son can do nothing by himself; he can do only what he sees his Father doing, because whatever the Father does the Son also does."** That is the way the father saw his relationship to his son.

And another verse from the Book of John:[81] **„Moreover, the Father judges no one, but has entrusted all judgment to the Son."**

The younger son was lucky that his father did not judge him. He would have had little chance to be forgiven. The older son was very far away from the relationship his father really would have liked to have with him.

It could be that the father says to his older son: "The whole situation is a lot worse than you think, dear son! To whom do the ring, the new clothes, the shoes belong to...? To you, the older son, as is told in Verse 12!

The older one is financing the rehabilitation of his younger brother! Works and slaves for the one who has returned to his home again.

Who will pay for the celebration? The older son! And he doesn't even take part! Through his decision and reaction, we see he had not yet accepted his part of the inheritance. If I do not accept my part of my inheritance, it will be given away, as a gift! I lost it! This is where faithful co-workers in churches and

_____

[79] Luke 10, 22

[80] John 3,35 and 5,19

[81] John 5,22

fellowships are in danger. They think they have to work and slave in order to keep the church, which is sometimes called a ship, from sinking! For whom? For God! But it could very well be without his explicit wish!

Our most important commission is to be his child. To stay very close to him. He will show us what his will is for us, after we have found out that we are children of our Father.

Verse 32

„But we had to celebrate and be glad, because this brother of yours was dead and is alive again; he was lost and is found."

We had to celebrate the one who has found his identity again, who found the way home.

Sometimes we could not celebrate over a big sinner, who had been in show business, in politics or somewhere else, very far away from the father, and then found the way to God.

Look at how much we have worked and slaved for Jesus and now he has entered the Kingdom of God! He didn't earn this!

That is true, but we didn't either! Because we cannot earn becoming the children of God the Father. To be filled with his life in his presence, near him. And no guilt in all the world can separate us from him. God took our guilt upon himself when Jesus died for our sins. Not „that son there of yours" but instead „he there, my son Jesus, carries the guilt". And for that reason we can come to the Father, as the younger son did, and be literally run over by the Father because of his joy over our return. And we do not have to earn this, as the older son tried to do.

God the Father loves us completely, including our needs for wearing a protective cover or holding up a shield before us or trying to be someone who we are not, all of which began in our childhood. He loves us as we are right now! But he doesn't leave it at that. God the Father leads us into our true commission, to be his son or his daughter.

He loves us just as much today as he loved us yesterday. And tomorrow not more nor less than today, no matter what we do. That he is saddened over things that we do, is another matter. But nothing can stand in the way of his love for me.

He is waiting to embrace us in his arms.

When does a child's life begin?
No – not at the moment of conception (Reading about Jesus and John the Baptist can explain this.[82]) It was instead when God the Father began to think about me and decided
that I should be Hans, or Maria with the personality I have. In the book of Ephesians is written:[83] „...before the creation of the world!" And then the Father thought about you for centuries. Our Father planned each of us, thought about us for thousands of years! Or, looking at it scientifically, which dates the origin of the world at 13,82 billion years ago, then for billions of years. We cannot fathom such time lengths, we are not capable of that. If I think about one person for more than 10 hours, I don't have any new ideas! But our Father in Heaven invested much more time! And finally you are here and he wants to talk to you about who you are and all the treasures and beauty and gifts he bestowed upon you.

Whether the Father wants to have children, or parents want to have children, is their decision. But when the children are born, the parents will be parents for the rest of their lives. A marriage can be divorced, an employment relationship can be cancelled, being a child will never end. When God the Father decided he wanted us, he agreed to be our Father for all of our lives; to be more exact, in all eternity!

Whether we see similarities between us and the younger or the older sons, each of us is as precious to God the Father as the other. Each child who does not sit on his lap he misses unbearably and looks continually day and night to see when we will finally come to him. No one can keep him from „eating his heart out" over us – he is Father in the deepest depths of himself.

---

[82] Luke 1,13 and 31
[83] Eph 1,4

An entrance ticket or fulfillment of some requirements to come to him are not needed. All we have to say is „Father, here I am." Really, that is all.

Jesus speaks in the book of John about his Father as Abba. This word means repetitive syllables, which children very often speak when learning how to form and articulate words. We do not have to speak well formed sentences to communicate with our Father; we can stutter the same sound time and again, which he dearly loves. The confession of our sins is the second step, but first I **must** experience the love of my Father. **His love** is what changes us - NOT the confessions of our sins!!

At times we think there are things which are in the way of us from coming to our Father, to whom Jesus wants to lead us. And there he has prepared a room for us. Have we begun to tell him what we want in our room? How it should look?[84] Perhaps a secret closet just for him and me?[85]

If there is something that is hindering me to come to my Father, I can ask the Holy Spirit to show me what that is.

Here we end, perhaps seeming abruptly, the second part of the Parable, as if the ending is missing or the original text is lost. We do not see this as the case. For the very next Parable[86] we will look at is about the unfaithful administrator. A contrast of daughters and sons who will always be ours, this administrator carries responsibility but ends up being unfaithful. In the end, he must leave, but children can always stay at home.

Because we are so important to God our Father, Jesus gave us this parable about the two very different children!
Both are precious to him.
Not only one out of a hundred,
Not only one out of ten,
each one!

---

[84] John 14,2
[85] Song of Solomon 5
[86] Luke 16,1-7

Perhaps we can summarize in this way:
Our theme is: Our Worthiness
Abba's theme: To have us with him
Like children in a family.
The family of God?

Part 2: ...his children ...

Being a child of my Father.

A great man is one who has preserved his childlike heart!
>   Mong Dsi (Chinese Philosopher 372-289 bef.Chr.)

It is never too late to have a happy childhood.
>   Ben Furmann (Finnish Psychiatrist)[87]

Only he who grows up and remains a child is a man.
>   Erich Kästner (Writer)[88]

God our Father wants to have a family.[89]

What? God our Father wants to have a family?

Yes, he actually had one before the beginning of the world.

A perfect family with Jesus and the Holy Spirit. Please don't have any cheap picture in mind, but rather let us see what became of this love

This is explained in the first three verses of the Old Testament :[90]

In the beginning God created the heavens and the earth.

This text speaks about God.

Now the earth was formless and empty, darkness was over the surface of the deep, and the Spirit of God was hovering over the waters.

These verses speak about God's Spirit, or as we call him, the Holy Spirit.

And God said:

This is the first time Jesus is mentioned as in the Prolog of the Gospel of John[91]:

„ In the beginning was the Word, and the Word was with God." Jesus is the Word of God.

"Let there be light," and there was light.

Jesus is the Light of the world. And he is seen by the world for the first time in

---

[87] Ben Furmann, Finnish Original published 1997 by WSOY, Juva, Finland: title: Ei koskaan liian myöhäistä saada onnellinen lapsuus"

[88] German writer of books for children like "Das fliegende Klassenzimmer", "Das doppelte Lottchen" und "Emil und die Detektive"

[89] look to chapter on The Lord's Prayer

[90] Gen 1,1-3

[91] John 1,1 ff

this text.

Before the universe was created, God had a perfect family: Father, Son and Holy Spirit. The Hebrew word for spirit is „ruach", a word of feminine gender. However this wasn't enough for the Father. He wanted to be surrounded by more people. He is so full of love that he has to give it to others.
Those who are in love know this feeling of wanting to embrace the whole world!

We cannot love alone. It has to have a counterpart, someone who will receive what we want to give.

God the Father was not able to hold back his love so he imagined how it would be to have living beings. And he created them. First of all the angels! Who serve him day and night. Who are always around him to live in joy and harmony with him.

But there was one angel who decided not to stay in his presence. That was Lucifer, the bearer of light, who was to bring light into his kingdom of the world. He was to precede Jesus, who is the Light of the World, but Lucifer himself was not that Light.
You are perhaps familiar with the Lucia-Celebration in Sweden and Norway, which takes place on December 13th, the winter solstice according to the Gregorian calendar. On this day the Return of Light is celebrated. This is when the sun returns after the period of total darkness in the northern hemisphere.

And so a young girl with a wreath of burning candles on her head comes into a completely dark room and fills it with light. Everyone is happy that it is not dark anymore!
Lucia brings light but she is **not** the light herself. The world is waiting for the Light of the World.

Back to our text: Lucifer was the one who was to bring light into the world. But HE wanted to be the Light himself, instead of Jesus, the son of God. For that reason he was banned out of heaven.

In the gospel of Luke there is a short verse about this:[92]
„He replied, "I saw Satan fall like lightning from heaven."

In the book of Ezekiel we can read these verses about Lucifer:[93]

12b "Son of man, take up a lament concerning the king of Tyre and say to him: 'This is what the Sovereign Lord says: " 'You were the seal of perfection, full of wisdom and perfect in beauty.

13 You were in Eden, the garden of God; every precious stone adorned you: carnelian, chrysolite and emerald, topaz, onyx and jasper, lapis lazuli, turquoise and beryl.2 Your settings and mountings3 were made of gold; on the day you were created they were prepared.

14 You were anointed as a guardian cherub, for so I ordained you. You were on the holy mount of God; you walked among the fiery stones.

15 You were blameless in your ways from the day you were created till wickedness was found in you.

16 Through your widespread trade you were filled with violence, and you sinned. So I drove you in disgrace from the mount of God, and I expelled you, guardian cherub, from among the fiery stones.

17 Your heart became proud on account of your beauty, and you corrupted your wisdom because of your splendor. So I threw you to the earth; I made a spectacle of you before kings.

18 By your many sins and dishonest trade you have desecrated your sanctuaries. So I made a fire come out from you, and it consumed you, and I reduced you to ashes on the ground in the sight of all who were watching.

19All the nations who knew you are appalled at you; you have come to a

---

[92] Luke 10,18
[93] Ezek 28, 12b - 19

horrible end and will be no more.' "

That is the story of why Lucifer was thrown out of heaven and became Satan –
an angel who became an opponent of God.

But then God decided to take a new chance, even though it could be risky:[94]

Then God said, "Let us make mankind in our image, in our likeness ."
We are made in the image of God, Jesus and the Holy Spirit and share a
familiarity with their fellowship as a family. Did you know that?

You look similar to your earthly father, however, you also have a similarity to
your heavenly father. This is more than what we wrote about God the Father in
chapter three.
Papa wanted to have us in his family. Between him, Jesus and the Holy Spirit.

Can we fathom what this means?!

This next verse emphasizes this aspect: Genesis 1, 27:
**So God created mankind in his own image, in the image of God he created
them; male and female he created them.**

What is interesting is that man and women both were made in his image.

Both reflect to others who God is.

This doesn't mean that we show all the different aspects and sides of our Papa.
Because a reflection is not reality. It doesn't show, for example, the sides and we
do not see the back. That means what should be three-dimensional is only two-
dimensional.

At home I have a magic mirror! Every time I look in it, I see someone. Myself.
And always at eye level. I have tried to quickly walk away, to bend over and
make myself small, to turn around, but my mirror always shows me at eye level.

---

[94] Gen 1, 26b

At eyelevel with Abba
This is what the text means. His children are always on eye level with him.

We are not God, Papa, who created heaven and earth.

But he wants to be on eyelevel with us. Just as his children.

Verse 31
God saw all that he had made, and it was very good. It was ALL good!

The stars, the oceans, the animals, the vegetation, everything was good.

But man and woman, they were very good.
God finally had a family.

But that was still not enough for him.

In Verse 28 the following is written:
„God blessed them and said to them, "Be fruitful and increase in number; fill the earth.„

So that he is surrounded by many, many children. By his children.

And he began to live with his family.

Just as he lived in heaven with his angels, he came down to earth to see Adam and Eve.
Every evening when the heat of the day slowly went away and the coolness of evening freshened the air.

That is when he came into the Garden of Eden to be with Adam and Eve.
Genesis 3, 8a:
„Then the man and his wife heard the sound of the Lord God as he was walking in the garden in the cool of the day."
To talk with them about their day.

To encourage them to begin with their jobs.

He showed them how to care for their garden.

Talked to them about their marriage. How were they to know how it should function?

They had quite a lot to ask him, just as little children bombard us with many questions.

What was burdening their heart.

And he was happy with his family.

But then the serpent came into the picture and sowed mistrust.

Fellowship can most easily be destroyed through mistrust.

Then Adam and Eve began to mistrust God the Father.

Is he really a good Father? asked the serpent.

No, answered the serpent himself. He is withholding something from you.

God doesn't want to give you everything.

I am the better Father, I will give you everything.

There is a tree in the middle of the garden.

And you are not allowed to eat from it!

The tree of the knowledge of Good and Evil.

Be not only at eye level with him, no: Become **like God!**

That was the secret wish of the serpent -to be like God.

That was the serpent's big lie: You will become like God. No, Adam and Eve would become as the serpent. It wants to be God and makes Adam and Eve the same as he is. Not God!

Eve was the first to get weak and Adam did not try to stop her! **He** was the one who God had told not to eat from this tree, not Eve![95] God must have told them because Eve knew it was forbidden to eat from the tree.[96]

The seed of mistrust however had already been sown!

Genesis 3, 6:

---

[95] Gen 2,17

[96] Gen 3, 2 - 3

„When the woman saw that the fruit of the tree was good for food and pleasing to the eye, and also desirable for gaining wisdom, she took some and ate it. She also gave some to her husband, who was with her, and he ate it.“

What was their first big realization?
They realized that they were naked.
WOW! That was worth having eaten from the tree.
Naked, not protected anymore through their trust in their Father.
Alone. At the mercy of the world.

How are we doing?

Is there anything which God has not given unto you?
Are there any situations in which you were not protected by God?
Why is there evil in the world?
Have all of your prayers been answered?

No!

Is he really a good Father?
Does he know what I need?
What my heart's desire is?
How I have been hurt und mistreated?
Is he really a good Father?

No?

We can look at all of this and ask „Do I deserve this?“
That others waste everything I had saved!
I do not deserve to be put off work or to get sick when I retire, after so many years!
No!

This is when we want to settle a score according to how we think things should be.

But it is a question of what kind of relationship we had as to whether or not we want to settle a score.

No one is going to hold it against a baby that it's diapers have to be changed at night. Where love and sympathy have the last word, the score is different! The more formal the relationship is, the more important is the settlement of the score.

Also and especially in the relationship to God the Father. The greater the decency, the more closely we observe the balance of giving and taking.

We need to know, though, that there are two levels in our life!

Level 1 is the world we live in. From the world's view, you are an adult. You behave like one, talk like one, work like one. Your understanding and your abilities are that of an adult. If you act like a child, people will laugh at you. The world calls that being childish. Not capable of meeting the responsibilities expected of you.

Putting forth effort is what we are asked to do. I have to fight for my place in the world. All that I need and must have can only be earned through my efforts. Without mercy or grace.

But there is also another level:

Level 2 is your relationship to Abba, about whom Jesus spoke.

In this relationship we are always like a 3-year old child.
Who expects his Father to provide all of his needs. And, of course, his mother; the Holy Spirit loves this job.

Three year olds do not make comparisons. Children at this age don't usually know what mistrust is. My father can do anything. That is the view of young children.

We are dependent upon our Papa and his love.
Without the love of parents, children's growth is stunted.
We need their love.

Without this love, the child within us dies.
And then, what is left inside, is only an adult shell.

However sometimes little children do not understand what their Father is doing.
He is like a stranger to them and hard to understand.

Here an example of our son Alexander.
He was allergic to pineapple. However one day, when he was around 3 years old,
he ate a piece. Within seconds he had a rash all over his body. Dark red blisters
all over. We rushed to the hospital.
The doctors had to give him a calcium injection.
But they couldn't find his veins. Time and again the doctor tried to make the
injection into a little vein, but it didn't work. I, Heinrich, was standing next to
him, holding his other hand. Alexander was crying and looked at me:
„Help me papa, they are mistreating me. Don't you see what they are doing to
me? Time and again and you are not doing anything about it? Why don't you
beat up the doctor?"
The only thing that I could do was to hold his other hand.

Finally they found the right vein. The allergic reaction disappeared right after
the injection.

He probably thought: My Father is here but he isn't helping me! I scream and he
does nothing. He is not caring for me. My father sees my pain, but he is not
saving me from it.

He could not understand his pain nor his Father.

Often we feel this way: God has not answered my prayers. I am sick, very sick. I
have lost something very precious to me. I have not been given something that I
so very much wanted. I am not getting what I need.

That is a very difficult moment.
That is a decisive moment.

In such a situation one moves to the other level. I leave the level of being a child that says: I trust my Father, even when I don't understand what he is doing now. ...and I move to the adult level. I have no control over the situation. God is neither doing what I want nor what I wish nor what I need. I have to get on top of this situation.

My neighbor was healed, why not I?
I had a terrible accident, why didn't he intervene?
I was mistreated, misused, why?
Am I really the child my God loves? This can't be the result of his love for me!

Jesus has something to say about this critical situation in Matthew 18, 2ff

2 He called a little child to him, and placed the child among them.

3 And he said: "Truly I tell you, unless you change and become like little children,   you will never enter the kingdom of heaven."

What does this mean? If you do not become a child of God, you will not enter the Kingdom of Heaven.

WOW!

Let's remember how Jesus reacted: His disciples pushed the mothers and children away who wanted to come to Jesus. The Greek word for this reaction is casting away, pushing away. They didn't just deny them the right to come, they aggressively prevented it!

Why did they do that? Because little Jewish children didn't have much worth from a religious point of view because they couldn't obey the Thora. They had to first learn how to do that. Around the age of 13 years the young boy became a member of the church.

„No", said Jesus, „unless you change and become like little children, you will not enter his Kingdom!" What does that mean?

Back to the level of a child. Back to the naive trust a 3-year old has in his Father. In spite of the situation, in spite of my condition. Why?

A child of this age doesn't know what it means to control. And that is the secret behind this. We want to have control over our lives. Best of all, with God's help. We want to understand and be in charge of our lives. But we lost that when the apple was eaten in the Garden of Paradise. At that time Adam and Eve lost their ability to trust as a child. And now we have the choice: Either find back to this childlike trust or master our lives ourselves. Some are very capable of this, others not so much. And still others not at all. That was not Abba's plan for us.

His plan is:
Come back and be my child again.
Tell me what you need!
Tell me what you long for!
Tell me what you would like to have.
Tell me what food, clothing, career, healing, forgiveness...you would like to have.
Tell me what your marriage partner, neighbor, friend, Father, Mother,
Pastor...should do. Or should not do.

Begin by trusting your Father.
The most important request in the Lord's Prayer is (look at chapter 12): „Give us this day, our daily bread". Our Father sees what we need. And what we need to live this day, he will give to us.
We can live as a little child that doesn't think about what it needs tomorrow. But lives in the present with its Father.

Even if we don't understand our circumstances nor our past life.

Even then, when it seems that he neither hears nor sees us..

Think about the story of my son Alexander! God the Father holds our hand!

Did you know that Abba took another big risk?

He came as a child into the world. He had to show us how to be a child of the Father.

Matt 1, 18-19
18 This is how the birth of Jesus the Messiah came about: His mother Mary was pledged to be married to Joseph, but before they came together, she was found to be pregnant through the Holy Spirit.

19 Because Joseph her husband was faithful to the law, and yet did not want to expose her to public disgrace, he had in mind to divorce her quietly.

Jesus was conceived outside of marriage. That is why his life and that of his mother were in great danger. In such a case as this, the mother would normally have been stoned.

Abba took care of both, as we can read in Verse 20 ff:

20 But after he had considered this, an angel of the Lord appeared to him in a dream and said, "Joseph son of David, do not be afraid to take Mary home as your wife, because what is conceived in her is from the Holy Spirit.
21 She will give birth to a son, and you are to give him the name Jesus, because he will save his people from their sins."

So Jesus was legally born:

That is described in Luke 2, 4 ff:
4 So Joseph also went up from the town of Nazareth in Galilee to Judea, to Bethlehem the town of David, because he belonged to the house and line of David
5 He went there to register with Mary, who was pledged to be married to him and was expecting a child.
6 While they were there, the time came for the baby to be born,
7 and she gave birth to her firstborn, a son. She wrapped him in cloths and placed him in a manger, because there was no guest room available for them.

Do you know what the most important statement is in these verses
„...**and wrapped him in cloths...**"!

That was the sign at that time that a child was born IN wedlock! Joseph must have been able to find the cloths. Maria had no money. God the Father took care that his son Jesus grew up in the protection of a married couple. Abba cares for his children.
That is what we celebrate at Christmas. He came as a child.
And he trusts us! That is why we can also trust him.
As his children.

Let us remember the last words Jesus cried out on the cross:
Luke 23,46:
„Jesus called out with a loud voice, "Father, into your hands I commit my spirit."
He commanded his Spirit what to do; it was an act of his will. It wasn't said out of despair or mistrust. He knew where he was commanding his spirit to go. Into the arms of his Father.

This is the mystery of our filiation, our child ship. His joy can then grow within us. Because we rest in his arms. That will change our lives! I do not have to understand what my Father has planned for me. I want to grow into what his will is for me. Not trying to control.
And let go of that which I do not understand - perhaps do not yet understand.

Kierkegaard once said:
„Life can only be understood backwards; but it must be lived forwards."
Live forwards as a child,
understand backwards as an adult.

Now I would like to pray for us:

Father, I thank you that we are your children.

93

Thank you for all that you have generously given to us.

Thank you that we belong to your Family. Wow!

Sometimes I don't understand you, Father.

I don't understand why you do some of the things the way you do.

That is at times very difficult.

It touches the depths of my heart.

But Father, I do not want to mistrust you.

I don't want to make the mistakes Adam and Eve made.

Right now it is just very hard.

Lift me up to my place with you, as your child.

A 3-year old child.

Who looks into the eyes of its Father.

So the child is sure that his Father knows what is happening.

I decide now to begin to trust you as my Father.

Amen

We ask you here, if you can, to speak the following prayer as your prayer.

Father,
I want to return to my child ship.
And not to stand before you as an adult.

But to be a child in your presence.

I trust that you know what is best for me.

I trust that you know what I need.

I trust that all good and bad will be used for a good purpose in my life.

All of this I entrust to you.

Father, I am so happy to be your child.

That will never end.

Thank you, Papa.

Amen.

There are some children, who belong to the child ship, but are not at home with their Father.

More about that in the following chapter.

No more an Orphan.

We have already talked about God wanting to have a family. Yes, he did have a family before he created the world: God the Father, Jesus and the Holy Spirit. Can't he just be God, all alone?

If God is a God of Love, he cannot be alone. We can't love by ourselves. Love must have a recipient.

Jesus wants to bring us into the Love of the Father.

With the following Bible verses we can look at this more in detail.

We can look at the Bible as the story of God and his relationship to his people. He wanted to have children who would have a different relationship with him than adults would. We tried to explain this in the last chapter. God the Father wanted more than just relationships: He wanted a family.

God had this plan for a very long time:

Let's look at John 14.

This is a wonderful story which goes along very well with the theme of a family.

In chapter 13 Jesus begins to prepare his disciples with the fact that he was going to leave them. That was the last thing his disciples would have expected! Jesus was going to leave them? What? That cannot be true!

So Jesus began to prepare them for that. And moreover, to strengthen their trust in him and his Father. How did he do that?

His disciples had lived with him for the last 3 years, as a family. They hiked together, experienced miracles together (Do you remember the Feeding of the 5000, the Calming of the Storm, the Healings that took place, walking on the water...), shared their lives with each other.

They sat with Jesus when he was with the sinners. Who are sinners? Easy to explain: People who are separated from God. Who are afraid of God. Because they separated themselves from him or they don't know anything about him. Do you remember the passage in Genesis when God came into the garden after

Adam and Eve had eaten the apple? [97] They were afraid. Before that, they were always together with God, now they hid and were afraid of him.

But Jesus was God too! Why were people not afraid of him? They were not able to imagine that God came upon the earth because he wanted to be with his children. Yes, Jesus loved being around sinners! Why? Because he was able to talk to them about his Father. They feared God, but not Jesus. They did though marvel at his teachings, which he told devotedly to them and at the power he had to heal. By the way, Jesus did not call the people to whom he spoke sinners. There are three identical passages in the Gospels where Jesus spoke about sinners while talking to the scribes.
Matthew 9, Mark 2 and Luke 5:
Luke 5, 32: „ I have not come to call the righteous, but sinners to repentance."
These words are his remark to the Pharisees, who had accused him of eating with sinners.

And now he wants to go away and leave his disciples. There is not only one reason for this: To die on the cross for our sins. We know that. And that will always be very vital.

In John 14 Jesus names three other reasons:
First: to prepare a place for us.
Second: He doesn't want to leave us behind as orphans.
Third: He will send us a helper and comforter, who will always be with us.

John 14,1:
„Do not let your hearts be troubled. You believe in God; believe also in me. Trust in God and trust in me!"

That is the greatest danger we are confronted with. We mentioned this theme in the chapter about the child. Perhaps we do believe, but to trust goes a big step further. The word „believe" comes from the root word „vow". I make a vow to someone, i.e., like an engagement. It has nothing to do with „to hold true"! And now we can think about the little child again. Jesus and his Father both say:

---

[97] Gen 3,10

Trust me.

Again: To trust is more than to believe something. To trust is more than hope. Trusting doesn't happen in our head, not in our heart but deep in our gut. Did you know that there are almost as many nerve cells in your gut as there are in your brain? Yes, that is right! That is what the Bible speaks of when we read about the heart. Not your beating heart, but your gut.

The deepest deep inside of you. That is your identity.

Scientists have made many investigations about how and where we make decisions. They have found out that our decisions are made in our gut, namely 0,3 seconds before our brain even reacts.

Our gut decides and our brain is given the job of logically reinforcing our decision.

If we trust Jesus from the depths of our gut, we become another person. Because it takes place deep within us!

We pray that you will allow Jesus to touch you there. And, deep within you, to put your trust in him.

Are you ready for such a decision? It is a decisive decision.

Be still for a moment and ask Jesus to be with you!

If you answered with „Yes", then I will pray for you now:

Lord Jesus, you know that we have a big problem in learning to trust you and your Father. Jesus, you know our desire to be able to trust you both.

Jesus, you heard our „Yes", softly spoken from deep inside.

Now I ask you, Jesus, to lay this trust deep within all those who have the desire to know you. For this is the beginning of all of our decisions to trust.

When trust is laid deep within you, then faith begins to grow and will, so to speak, turn your heart and your mind upside down!

Jesus, I want to trust you.

I ask you to please enter my life, deep within me.

That will bring calmness and your peace, Jesus, into my soul.

And your peace, Father.

Amen

Holy Spirit, in your name I seal that which has happened within me. Please imprint this deeply into our souls:
The trust of a little child in its Father.
For we need this desperately.

Thank you, Holy Spirit. AMEN

Trust is the beginning of Faith. Not the result. Trust is the beginning of Faith.

Now to John 14,2:
„My Father's house has many rooms; if that were not so, would I have told you that I am going there to prepare a place for you?"

My Father's house has many rooms. First of all: God our Father has a house. We don't have to build one for him. Even the Temple in Jerusalem was the footstool for his feet. A church is also not his home. It isn't a concrete silo, an apartment on the 12th floor, the 54th row, at the back.
No, a king has a palace!
Have you ever been to the Palace of Versailles near Paris? A beautiful building with 1000 rooms. But our Father can top that!
He has a house for all of his children. In his house we are safe, protected against rain, hail and snow, the cold and the heat and, most important, against evil. And we are always welcome.
It isn't a guest house or a hotel, which we must leave some day. No, it is the house of our Father. We live there as his children, not as adopted or foster children. No, as full-fledged citizens, as Paul said.[98] As beloved children of our Father.

For there are MANY rooms in his house. Not an apartment that is overcrowded. No, there is a room just for you. There is a room which only you and your Father

_____

[98] Eph 2,19

are allowed to enter. A private room. Did you know that your Father has a nick-name for you? For each of us? Ask him! He told me what his nickname is for me! And he has a room for you, just as you would like for it to be. Furnished and decorated exactly as your heart desires. We should tell Jesus and our Father what our wishes are. Which color, which furniture, a ceramic tile or a wooden floor,...

We must tell Jesus, the craftsman, what we want!

Jesus continues in Verse 2:

„If that were not so, would I have told you that I am going there to prepare a place for you?"

Jesus is preparing a place for me. You know that Jesus learned the trade of a carpenter from his father. He certainly knows how to build a house.

And he wants only the best for you!

That was a further reason for him to come to earth. To see with his own eyes what it means to be a human being. Jesus knows about all the problems people have with each other. Sometimes we think God has no idea what is happening here on earth. But Jesus does know.

Here we have something important to say about Islam and about Mohammed:[99]

As Mohammed was dying, his daughter Fatima was sitting beside his bed and asked him: „Father, you are dying. But where are you going and what will happen to us?"

Mohammed said to her: „You can ask me for all of my wealth but I cannot save you from the wrath of Allah. I swear to Allah, although I am his disciple, but I don't know what Allah will do with me."

That is THE difference between Allah and Jesus and what he does for us. Jesus knew where he would go and where he would take us when we die.

And Jesus continues:

Verse 3:

And if I go and prepare a place for you, I will come back and take you to be

---

[99] Source Joel-News 2012 Edition 19

with me that you also may be where I am.

When all the rooms are finished for his disciples. For the Father's children. And the Father is happy about what his son is doing. Then all of his children will be with him.

This promise was made in Psalm 23.[100] Surely goodness and mercy will follow me all the days of my life and I will dwell in the house of the Lord forever.

And you know what? I can stay there. No one will try to take my room away from me! Once and for all, peace!

Back to the text.

Verse 6:

Jesus answered, "I am the way and the truth and the life. No one comes to the Father except through me."

To follow Jesus means to be on the way to our Father!

Jesus is not the big goal.

That is the Father!

There are many ways to find to Jesus but only one way to the Father.

And Jesus is the way.

But what happens in the meantime?

While Jesus is working on our room?

The time between now and then?

We find the answer in Verse 18:

 I will not leave you as orphans; I will come to you.

Orphans.

They have neither mother nor father.

Because they either died or just abandoned their children.

An orphan is all alone in the world.

No one cares for them.

No one loves him or her.

No one needs an orphan.

---

[100] Psalm 23,6

An orphan is useless.

In Africa there are many „dumped children". The father or the mother do not want them anymore because they are in the way of a new relationship. So they are dumped off at the grandparent's home. They have become a burden. How do these children feel when they are dumped off?

The only chance an orphan has is to take care of itself.
And we do that.
Like an orphan.
No one takes care of me.
No one is interested in me.

And I will get everything that I can.
I'll steal, if necessary.
I want more.
I never have enough.
My hands will tightly grip all of my possessions.
I won't give anything to anyone.
I want to have everything that I need right now – Fast-food mentality!

All of my needs have to be fulfilled in my relationships.
If that isn't possible, then I will just leave you and try my luck with someone new.
But the crux of the matter is - I am the source of my problem!
And I will take the problem, which is me, with me into the next relationship.

And orphan once said:
Don't trust anyone, then they only want something from you.
Don't trust anyone, because they will cheat you.
Think about all the dangers around you.
Life is giving you a hard time.

That is the spirit of an orphan.
All of mankind has this spirit since we lost Paradise.
The spirit of an orphan, who is alone in the world.
Who is only interested in relationships, if there is something in it for themselves.

That is the greatest danger for Christians.

God is a mighty God.

He can give us everything.

He has everything.

I would be stupid, not to be a Christian!

Because I can get everything which I need.

After all, I am a poor orphan.

Jesus knew this because he had exactly the same experience when he was on earth.

Ten Lepers were healed by him, only one returned and thanked him for this miracle.[101]

People saw the miracles he performed, they were excited by what they saw and wanted more.[102]

Or the miracle of the vineyard which was rented to others. The Tenants decided to kill the son so they could have more.[103]

Jesus looked and knew what was happening.

And then he made a big promise.

„I will never leave you alone as orphans.“

Orphans, who have no personal relationships.

But instead business on mutual terms.

Or by contract: I will give a small amount and you have to give me much more.

But how can we overcome this spirit?

Verse 16:
And I will ask the Father, and he will give you another advocate to help you and be with you forever.

Jesus asks his Father for help. To whom else will the Father listen to, if not to his

_____

[101] Luke 17, 12-16
[102] Matthew 12 and 16
[103] Luke 20, 1-16

son Jesus!

And his Father knows that.

And Papa has a solution.

He sends another Helper!

The Holy Spirit!

Jesus was the first helper. He showed us who the Father is, as he is described in the last few verses.[104]

However Jesus had to leave so that the Holy Spirit could come to his Father's children.

And he, the Holy Spirit, will stay with us forever!

Verse 17:

The father will give you the Spirit of truth. The world cannot accept him, because it neither sees him nor knows him. But you know him, for he lives with you and will be in you.

The following is very important:

1.The Holy Spirit is the Spirit of Truth.

This means: Lies and untruth cannot exist next to him. Like two magnets which bump each other off and cannot come together.

The Holy spirit will lead you to the truth which your Father knows about you. Since the beginning of the world.

And this truth will make you free.

Because there are no lies or untruths in it.

The Holy Spirit is the connecting link between us and God the Father.

2. The Spirit of Orphans is the Spirit of Controlling. An orphan has to have everything under control. With itself, in marriage, the family, the job and even in the church.

A prince or a princess – that is who we are as children of the King of Kings, and we have others to help us. In Greek „parakletos", which means the one who was called to help. It is he, the Holy Spirit, who can do that much better: In the first verse of the Bible we read: He was hovering over the waters. He was planning and creating all that the Father wanted to have here on earth. The Hebrew word

---

[104] John 14, 6-8

„ruach" is feminine; the Holy Spirit can be seen as the feminine side of God.
We cannot be filled with the Holy Spirit and at the same time have control over others.

3. It is important to know that Truth and Facts are not the same. You all know the story about Abraham and Sarah in the Old Testament. The fact was that Sarah was 90 years old and could definitely not have any more children.
For generations!
The truth is that she bore Isaac at the age of 90!

The established facts of your life are not the **truth** about you. The truth is what our Father sees in you.
The truth is that the Father sees you as his beloved child. He smiles and laughs when he sees you.
At this moment!
Right now!
Like the prodigal son in Luke 15.
He saw his beloved child.
And it is one of the most important things that the Holy Spirit works in us – that we are convinced of this in our hearts.
No, it has to go deeper, into your gut, way down inside.
You are that beloved child of the Father.
And that is why we need the Holy Spirit so urgently. Because we cannot convince ourselves of this alone.

And Jesus promised to send him.

The world cannot receive the Holy Spirit!
Why?
Because the world can neither feel nor know anything about him.
There is a different spirit in the world.
The spirit of an orphan.

The Holy Spirit and the spirit of an orphan cannot exist next to each other.
Perhaps the spirit of an orphan was helpful to you at the beginning of your life, to help you keep living. But he is a big hindrance now and can keep you from

experiencing the love of our Father.

So we can make a choice.
We can send the spirit of an orphan away and invite the Holy Spirit to dwell in us.

Do I want that?

If not yet, the Holy Spirit will wait. Jesus will wait. The Father will wait and hope.

If we do decide for his Spirit, if this wish comes from the depth of your heart, then I will pray for us now:
Lord Jesus, I pray for protection through your blood.

I place all of you under the protection of the blood of Jesus.
And all who belong to us and all of our possessions.
Jesus, you will now take care of all of this.

I speak now to you, Spirit of an Orphan.

I proclaim in the Name of Jesus, that you have no right to stay in these children of the Father.
Please speak the following words out loud:
In the name and according to the order of Jesus I separate myself from this spirit of an orphan.
I am not an orphan anymore.
You, Spirit of an Orphan, have no more power over me.
I am a beloved child of my Father.
Holy Spirit, I invite you to take over the room within me which is only there for you.

Amen.

Lord Jesus, according to your order and in your name I command right now this orphan spirit to leave the beloved children of God the Father.

I command him through the given authority of Jesus, that he must go to the place which Jesus will direct him to and must stay there.

I set you all free from this spirit, his power is at an end. His right over you has been nailed to the cross.

And now I ask you, Hoy Spirit, to fill all the room which the orphan spirit had unlawfully filled.
Come and fill the beloved children of the Father.
Come and fill them with yourself.
And transform these people from orphans to children of the father. Begin this work right now.

Encourage their trust.
Father, I thank you for the miracle you are performing.
I thank you, Holy Spirit, for your presence.

Amen.

Now to our highest privilege in the New Testament!

Adoption

We tend to emphasize that we are justified before our Father through Jesus and that is right. However the adoption through Jesus' Father is the culmination of our salvation in the Bible.
We have been adopted by our Father!

Paul speaks of this four times in his letters.[105]

We don't really think of this as something sensational. It's just the opposite: adoption is a second-class relationship, the own biological children will always have the first-class relationship.
But Paul used this example because he knew the rights of Roman citizens since he was one himself.[106]
The letters in which he wrote about adoption were written to churches in the Roman Empire, for the recipients knew about the process of an adoption according to Roman laws.
Jesus talked also about our Father's acceptance of us, but he did not use the word adoption. Why not? Adoption was not a part of the Jewish laws and to make comparisons with the Romans was not such a wise thing to do, as the Romans would not have accepted it.

What makes these laws of adoption[107], which Paul uses as an example, so special? It is far from our adoption laws of today in Germany, even though ours are based upon the Roman laws of adoption.

Let us take a look at the rights of biologically born children: According to Roman law, the father had the right of disposal over his children. He had the right to dispel them, sell them into slavery, even to kill them, which often happened if daughters were born. The biological children in a family were not at all in a secure position. This was the same in the Greek culture. Contrary to our

---

[105] Eph 1,5: Gal 4,5; Romans 8;15; 9,4
[106] Acts 16 and 22
[107] Charles Welch, Just and the Justifier, the Berean Publishing Trust, London, Page 212, more explantations on pages 208 - 213

understanding and the administration of justice in Germany.

Now to adopted sons (we'll handle daughters later):
The process of adoption was complicated and encompassed many different factors in which the original family of the child, the health, height, bodily strength, character and education played a decisive role.
Usually the reason for adoption was that there was no suitable male offspring for the continuation of the family or the business. Adoption is a legal process with rules to be exactly followed. In contrast to salvation, which was a term used in the healing arts. Here we are talking about adoption as a legal process which had to exactly fulfill legal laws.

Paul gives us an important statement about the process of selection by his Father:
Eph 1,14: „For he (our Father) chose us in him (Jesus) before the creation of the world to be holy and blameless in his sight." (Luther translation 84)
The process of selection made by our Father was finished before he created the world. **That is incomprehensible !** The plan for our adoption had always been a part of the plans of creation! Before we were born, our Father already wanted to adopt us! We **ARE** holy and blameless before Him! We passed our selection procedure!
We passed it before we were even born!
What a Father!

Ephesians 1, 4b + 5:
In love he predestined us for adoption to son ship through Jesus Christ, in accordance with his pleasure and will. (Translation: New International Version)

However the one who will be adopted must be in agreement! It isn't an agreement of sale, as if a slave was to be sold. He or she can make their own choice. Since being adopted in the Roman Empire was a step up the social ladder, the decision was easy to make. The one to be adopted probably didn't understand what all this step would bring for them. Similar to the decision to give one's life to Christ, although a child of the world becomes a child of the King!

It is important to look at the legal consequences of being adopted according to Roman law:

The old family lost all rights over the person to be adopted, all the debts were deleted and all dependencies were over with. The adopted person had absolutely no more ties to the old family and was integrated into the new family. The one adopted **did not have the right** to cancel the decision; it was final, just as the paternity of a biological child can never be reversed.

Save alone the adopted one decided to leave the family and carried through with their decision. But he was also not a child of his first family either! That meant that adopted children had more security in the family than the biological children of the family. That has unbelievable consequences on our relationship to our Abba Father! We are absolutely secure and safe with him! He will never delete our adoption! Never!!

Four big changes came into the lives of those who were adopted:
A new family.
A new name.
A new home.
New tasks.

What does that mean for us?

We become a member of a **new family**, the family of God. We are taken into the loving relationship between the Father, Jesus and the Holy Spirit. Everything that was a part of our life, has no more power over us. All of our guilt and intrigues are gone. All the past is gone.

Baptism is an example of what happens by to us by adoption to our heavenly Father. Symbolically all of our past is submerged in the water and dies. Jesus' command to us in Matthew 28,14 says: "..and baptize them **IN** the name of the Father and the Son and the Holy Spirit." We are baptized **INTO** the family of God.

Our **new name** is Child of God. Our family name isn't anymore a "worldly name", but is now "God's child"! The Scandinavian and Arabian languages have kept this way of naming their children. Sigurdson means son of Sigurd; Sigurdotor means

111

daughter of Sigurd. Or Ben Ali means son of Ali. And among the Jews it was so: Jesus was called Jesus Bar Joseph, Jesus, son of Joseph. No one is allowed to call us by our old name.

Jesus talked about our **new home** in John 14. He prepared a new room for us in his Father's house. And more than that, the Father, Jesus and the Holy Spirit live **IN** us (John 17, 21-23).

New tasks.
Our tasks as Princes and Princesses are different from those of subjects. We don't have to fight to survive, don't have to pay off any debts. And what is even more wonderful is that the door to our King, our Father, is always open! If we peek into the Throne Room and he sees us, he sends away his dignitaries so he can take time with his children.

Another word about Jesus.
To put it another way: God sacrificed his biological son in order to adopt us. Jesus paid the price for our adoption. He eradicated our guilt and solved all of our confusions and entanglements. That is what he legally did for us, which at the same time, brought us our salvation.
What a Father!

A short word to the daughters.
Is Paul sexist because he did not mention daughters?
NO!
The right to be adopted was only for young boys and men. Had Paul spoken about sons and daughters, he would have weakened his statement. But Paul was more radical: he called men and women "Sons" of God, just as angels are neither male nor female. He wanted to say in this way that Christian women and men have the same status, even though the culture of that time did not agree. (Galatians 3,28)

This was made known in the Old Testament in Isaiah 56, 3ff:

3 "Let no foreigner who is bound to the Lord say, "The Lord will surely exclude

me from his people." And let no eunuch complain, "I am only a dry tree."
4 For this is what the Lord says: "To the eunuchs who keep my Sabbaths, who choose what pleases me and hold fast to my covenant—

 5 to them I will give within my temple and its walls a **memorial and a name better than sons and daughters**; I will give them an everlasting name that will endure forever."

In the book of Acts the Eunuch, the court official, the financial minister from the Ethiopian Queen Candace, experienced this and was **therefore** the first heathen to become a Christian!

About Man.

After having looked at the similarities of the children of the Father and the privileges of adoption, we will now look at the Man and the Woman. In this chapter we begin with the man.

Women will probably be just as interested in this chapter as the men. Perhaps to better understand your husband or your boyfriend. Or to better understand the difficulties you are having with him.

Perhaps you will be able to understand some reasons.

If you have the need to delve deeper into this theme, I recommend you to read the book "Wild at Heart" from John Eldredge.[108]

We want to look at three things:
What is a man?
What do men have to do?
Which big jobs does the Father have for men?

Let's go to the beginning of the Bible, the first verses of the Creation:
Genesis 1,27:
So God created mankind in his own image, in the image of God he created them; male and female he created them.

So the first thing God the Father did was to create man and woman according to his image: some translate it so: In his image. He laid something of himself into each one, in the man and the woman.

Looking at them together gives us a better picture of what God's plan was with them. And that was what marriage is and means. An idea, a small picture of the Holy Trinity, who God the Father is.

That would be a good theme for a book about marriage. However we have to concentrate now on the man.

We must keep the following in mind as we begin:
The man was created first!
We can read about this in Genesis 2,4b to 7:

---

[108] John Eldredge, Wild at Heart, Thomas Nelson Inc.

4b when the Lord God made the earth and the heavens.

5 Now no shrub had yet appeared on the earth and no plant had yet sprung up, for the Lord God had not sent rain on the earth and there was no one to work the ground,

6 but streams came up from the earth and watered the whole surface of the ground.

7 Then the Lord God formed a man from the dust of the ground and breathed into his nostrils the breath of life, and the man became a living being.

This means that the man was created in the wilderness. Out of wet dust. And there, life was breathed into him, he was kissed into life.
This did not happen in the Garden of Eden!
In verse 8 is written:
Now the Lord God had planted a garden in the east, in Eden; and there he put the man he had formed.
Later on in verse 21 to 23 Eve is created, we will come back to that.

Created in the wilderness!
To be exact: in Africa.
What?
In Africa?
Scientists have found out that all people living today have their origin in Africa. And it was found out by examining the DNA. The written name is DEOXYRIB NUCLEIC ACID.

That is our construction plan, just for me, and no one else (except identical twins) has the same plan!
In America one can have their DNA analyzed to see where their male ancestors came from, how they came to Europe or the rest of the world! On hand from typical changes in the pictures of the lowest cells, it is possible to go back to their ancestors.
That functions with women too, but only with the female line.

Here is what was found out about me, Heinrich:

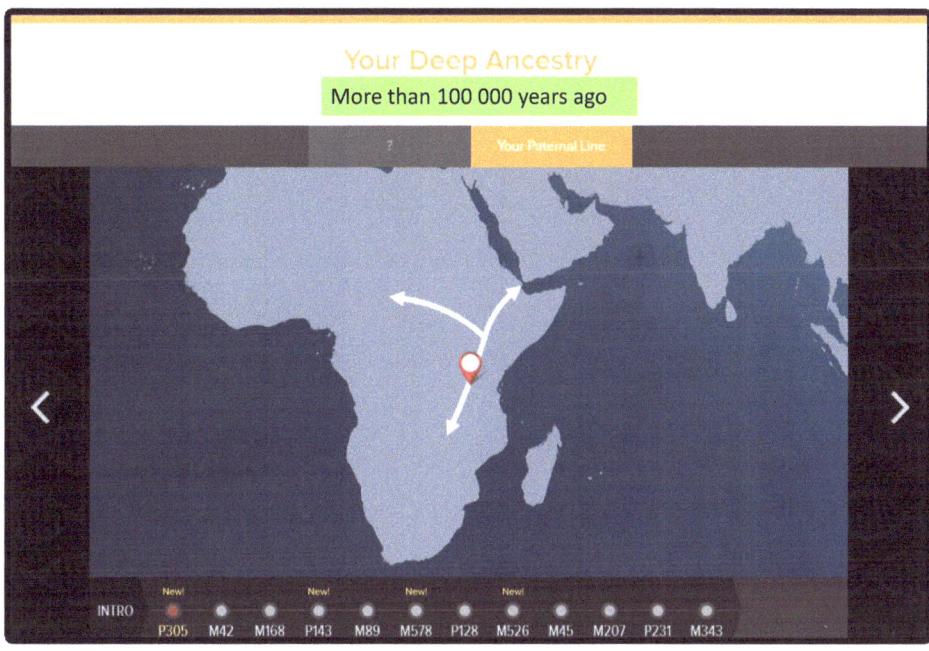

My ancestors went north first, then went out of the way through Asia:

A comment about this:
My ancestors went through Babel, perhaps they even helped build the Tower of Babel.[109]
And then, as all peoples, each went their own way.

---

[109] Genesis 11

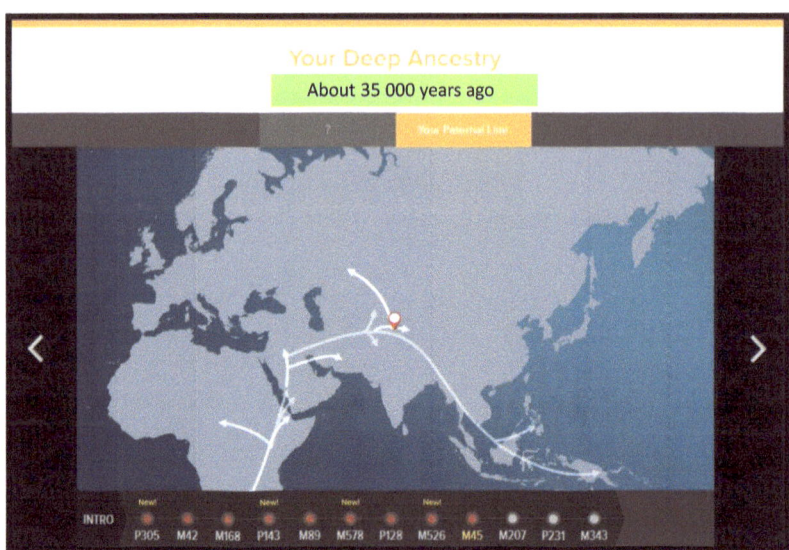

And then finally landed in Europe.

That means, my great-, great-, great-, great......Grandfather came from Africa.
Born in the wilderness.

118

All living men from today can trace their ancestors back to one man from Africa. And he came from the wilderness.

And I do believe that this fact has a big influence upon my and your soul, as a man. How we behave as men. How we react as men. Which talents, characteristics have been given to us.

The first men were hunters for thousands of years, before they settled down. We can successfully observe that even today.
During the last World Soccer Tournament I was in a bar. It was full of men (and also a few women!). They screamed when a goal was made. They moaned when the ball went to the side. Just like hunters.
They felt like they were part of the challenge, even though they were so far away.
That is the world of men.
Challenges, adventures, big tasks.

Just as Adam experienced.
Have you ever read about the huge task Adam had to complete before he got married?
Genesis 2,19-20a:
19 Now the Lord God had formed out of the ground all the wild animals and all the birds in the sky. He brought them to the man to see what he would name them; and whatever the man called each living creature, that was its name.
20a So the man gave names to all the livestock, the birds in the sky and all the wild animals.

An unbelievable task!
Do you know how many different species of butterflies are known about today? 160 000 different species! And every year researchers find around 500 new ones!

More than 100 000 different species of birds, more than 5400 species of mammals.

And Adam found a name for each of the animals. He didn't number them, as we

119

number stars – no, names. No one would be able to do that today. And no one knows all the animals in the oceans. 80% of them are unknown!

A tremendous task.
And men love big tasks.
More than that, they need big tasks.
Otherwise they wouldn't become a man.
They must be able to take grips with a huge task.

Here are a few examples from the Bible:

- Abraham wandered for thousands of miles through the desert to the land that was promised to him – The Promised Land.
- Moses led the people of Israel out of Egypt, through the desert for 40 years, after which they reached the Promised Land.
- Joshua led the conquest of the Promised Land.
- David defended his country in innumerable battles.

- And finally Jesus:

He had two big tasks:
1.   To tell about his Father and to lead his disciples into a relationship with him and his Father. Before he was crucified Jesus prayed:
„ I have brought you glory on earth by finishing the work you gave me to do."[110]
2.   To save men and women who had lost their relationship with the Father. Yes, Jesus came into the world to save sinners.[111]

And he succeeded!
Even then, when people thought he had failed because he was crucified and nailed to the cross and died.
But his Father raised him up from the dead! That was the greatest victory in the history of mankind.
After the greatest adventure in the history of mankind, which is, to be exact,

---

[110] John 17,4
[111] 1. Tim 1, 15

that God himself came into the world.

All men and women can now enter the Kingdom of God.

Do you know the task your Father has for your life?

And that for which he has prepared you?

It probably isn't just one task, but many, one after the other.

If not, then ask the Holy Spirit, he will tell you. Step by step.

Whether or not you are successful in your own eyes, or those of the world, is not important!

It is very important to start your task with the help of the Holy Spirit.

That will give you satisfaction and peace.

However, not the tasks we pick out for ourselves! No matter how Christian they may seem.

No, our Father has tasks for us, which exceed our imagination.

Back to Adam in Genesis:

After his first adventure and his great task, he needed a helper.

Helper – although:

Helper is not the correct translation.

In the French translation we read: il ne trouva pas d'aide qui soit son vis-à-vis.[112]

Translated it means: He found no helper who would talk face to face with him.

In Hebrew we find the word EZER KNEGDO. Translated it means: I will give him a helper, comparable to him. A helper has his own opinions. (The Holy Spirit is the Parakletos, one called upon to help. He certainly has his own opinion.) A helper is not a slave. No employee. But someone comparable to the other. We will return to this later.

Eve was created in the Garden of Eden. But not from a rib. Any man would have overcome losing a rib, he has 12 pairs of them. We men would be able to carry that loss.

Here's a joke about this:

God made the woman first, wonderful, very beautiful, Adam was overwhelmed.

---

[112] Bible du Sémeur 1999, French translation of the Bible

Adam asked: How much does she cost? God answered: One of your legs. Adam then asked: What do I get for one of my ribs?

No, the translation is: From him, from his side!
He was just not complete without her. And she surely wasn't either! That is why Paul wrote:
„Submit to one another out of reverence for Christ."[113]

Back to Genesis 2,22:
God brought her to him.
That was the first marriage ceremony. God the Father is the founder of marriage. He brought Eve to Adam!
And Adam was thrilled! He was full of joy and cried out: „Finally! It's her! Just like me!"[114]

Let us take some more time with these thoughts. Every time something is in the Bible for the first time, we must be concentrated to the utmost.
For here we find the first task for men in marriage.

Genesis 2,24:
„ That is why a man leaves his father and mother and is united to his wife, and they become one flesh."

The first task for the man is: To leave his father and mother.
Why does he have to do that and not the woman?
In those days, when a woman had gotten married, she always left the house of her father and mother. Think about Isaac and Rebecca, who came from far away to be with him and never saw her family again. No letters, no email, no telephone, no WhatsApp. Her family had disappeared from her life. She was only allowed to bring her nurse with her.[115]
Or look at Jacob with Rachel and Leah. Both women never went back into their father's house.

---

[113] Eph 5,21
[114] Translation Good News
[115] Gen 24,59

In the New Testament in the Parable of the ten young virgins we find the same situation.[116] The virgins accompanied the bride to the house of her groom, where she was to stay.

Now to the Groom!
He built an additional room in his father's house.[117] That means he stayed in his father's house. Though he had a room for himself and his wife, his father and mother were always around them. If he was still emotionally tied to his father or mother, how could the marriage be fruitful and stabile?
We don't want to delve into stories about the ugly mother-in-law, however the influence of a mother can be enormous if no borders are drawn.

My, Heinrich, relationship to my mother was very difficult for a long time. My parents got a divorce when I was 4 years old. At that time a divorce was only possible if the one or other was guilty. My father turned out to be the guilty one for he had relationships with other women during their marriage and especially when my mother was pregnant with my sister, who was 2 years younger than I. My mother always thought the way my father treated her   was a great injustice and began to hate him. To forgive him was impossible for her, although she later remarried and even celebrated her Silver Anniversary with my good stepfather. For this reason it is necessary and good for men to work through their thoughts and experiences they had with their fathers!
Of course what I had experienced had a big influence upon my picture of a father. Whenever something didn't turn out as my mother had wanted, she would say: „You are just like your father." That was definitely meant to be negative and made me very insecure, because I for sure knew how a man should not be. I did not even work through this part of my life for many years after I had become a Christian.
As my mother once again used these words, the Holy Spirit told me how to answer: „You chose my father, not I!" This incident was the beginning of an emotional separation from my mother; and now because I was able to forgive her, this chapter is closed.
My father remarried also but died in the middle of the 1970s. I also worked

---

[116] Matt 25,1
[117] Psalm 19,5; Song of Salomon 1,4

through my relationship with him and forgave him for not giving me what I'd needed as a young man. And today I miss him.

So, the first task a man should complete before he gets married is to emotionally separate himself from his parents. And to accept the task of caring for his wife; not being responsible for his wife, as we will see in chapter 11. Here's what Paul had to say about marriage:[118]

„Husbands, love your wives, just as Christ loved the church and gave himself up for her."

„In this same way, husbands ought to love their wives as their own bodies. He who loves his wife, loves himself."

Love your wife. That is an unbelievable task. Love her, just as the Father and Jesus loves the man.

Paul goes on to say:" and to present her to himself as a radiant church, without stain or wrinkle or any other blemish, but holy and blameless."[119] And buying her beautiful clothes is part of his task. To love your wife means: Take care of her. Even more: Give up yourself for her. She is your main task here on earth.

Wow!

To give yourself for her. Just as Jesus did.

That is another very big task for the man: Love your wife. Not only for the first ten minutes after you have gotten married. That means working on and investing in the relationship. What is Paul trying to tell us? To see the wife as a God-given task for my life.

Now back to Genesis 2, we have another comment.

The second part of the verse Genesis 2,24:

And they became one flesh. A more correct translation says: They were glued together. Whoever has glued two pieces of wood together, knows that the two pieces cannot be separated without some harm being done to the wood. They are so well glued together that one could think they are together one piece. Finally Adam's missing piece is part of him again. They are now one flesh. Their decisions are made jointly. They are One. They are looked at by God as if they

---

[118] Eph 5, 25 + 28
[119] Eph 5,27

were only one person.

This all has also another aspect:

When a man or a woman has sexual contact with a partner, they remain one flesh with this person. It could be that my opinion is not accepted in this day and time, but it is biblically based.

Paul emphasized this again in 1. Corinthians 6,16. That would be a good theme for a book about marriage.

It is even more serious if the one or other partner experienced sexual abuse before their marriage. We consulted with a man who had been married for 30 years but was bound to his mother because of sexual abuse. With the help of the Holy Spirit we were able to release him from the bondage to his mother. After this experience he told us about a prophesy he had been given many years ago: There is a wrong glue in your marriage.

Finally both of the partners understood what the prophesy's message was!

By the way, the Father created ONE woman.

Not several ones, from whom Adam could make his own choice. Nowhere in the Bible can we find any passages which tell us that Adam had thought about divorce or separation. He decided to live with this woman. That is marriage. Until death separates them. There was no competition. He didn't look to the left or to the right. His heart was not divided. He had no other option. That is the basis of a strong and healthy marriage.

(We do not want to deny that in some marriages positively growing and developing is not possible anymore. In such cases it is necessary and merciful to separate. This exemption though is not the rule.)

Back to the time after they were married:

After awhile the man becomes a father. Here we can learn from Abba Father what is and how to be a father. Ask him how a man can become a father as Abba wishes from the bottom of his heart.

By the way, this is not only meant for married men. This is meant for the task of being a single man also.

This means, first of all, that a father remains father of his children for all of his life! This „contract" cannot be annulled. Even if the children should turn away. How many times has Abba Father experienced this!!

A father cares for his children, prays for them, teaches them, provides all their needs: love, a home, upbringing, food, education…

The best thing that a man can do for his children is to love their mother.

That gives the children a secure and healthy atmosphere in which they can grow up.

Now just a few remarks about the differences in the upbringing of girls and boys. First of all I must say that both are equal, but not similar.

To the boys: (more about the girls in the next chapter)

„Then our sons in their youth will be like well-nurtured plants."[120]

A son is a gift of Abba Father. A young plant, which a father must help to grow and develop. In viniculture the idea of „raising" the grapevine to have different characteristics, according to where it is grown and the type of grapevine it is, is decisive.[121]

This chapter should not become a book about the upbringing of boys, but we do want to emphasize what is important to us.

First of all, the son should not be a copy of his father. He should not try to make up for what I did not achieve or become. Nor what others expect of him.

The most important thing (I am using thoughts of John Eldridge here), is that I can tell him as his father: He is a man! That he has all the characteristics and strengths of a man. No one other than a man can tell him this – not a comrade nor a friend, and surely not a woman.

Best of all is to be told by his own Father!

He will master his life! He will find out what his life's tasks are from Abba Father. He will be a good father to his sons, should he have any. He will be a good husband for his wife. And will tell his daughter how valuable she is!

Many fathers fail here. Who can tell this to their son, if they have left the mother and the children? How can a single mother do this?

Here also I will enter the gap left after your father deserted you and make up for what he neglected. I pray:

---

[120] Ps 144, 12a

[121] Keyword „Rebziehung" in Wikipedia.de

Abba Father
In your name I say to the reader of this book:
You are a man of God the Father.
You will master your life.
I bless you with the abilities you need to find your task for your life, which your Abba Father has prepared for you.
You are a beloved son of Abba Father.
You are a man after the heart of God.
Amen.

Perhaps someday you will be a grandfather. Now while we are writing this book, we are becoming grandparents for the second and third time. A wonderful time of waiting!

The first task of a grandfather is to make a connection to the past for the grandchild.
I can remember the stories my grandfather told me, who was a farmer, who knew everything about horses and was a talented craftsman. And how he would tell about the war! He was in the First and Second World Wars. We must tell our grandchildren how things were when we were young. Und all the pranks we played! And how it was in those days without telephone, computer and apps. And we can spoil them when their parents are not around.
That is a wonderful time in the life of a man and I look forward to seeing my future grandsons and granddaughters.

There is one more task about which we need to speak.
To pass on your blessing
It is very moving to read how Jacob blessed his sons:[122]
For each son he had a different blessing. He took consideration of the characteristics and talents of each son.
And then the very special blessing which Jacob gave to his grandchildren.[123]

---

[122] Gen 49,
[123] Gen 48, 13-22

In spite of the placement of names which Josef used, Jacob was careful of what Abba Father wanted and crossed his hands! He favored Ephraim the younger before the older Manasseh. Similar to Israel (Isaac), the younger son of Abraham, who was favored over Ishmael, the older son.

So ask the Holy Spirit which blessing you should lay upon your children and grandchildren.

And there is a very special blessing for the first born child. You perhaps know the story about how Jacob tricked his father into giving him the blessing which was meant for Esau, his first-born son.[124] And Isaac could not cancel the blessing! Which was a very special blessing, meant for the first born child.

Summary:
The biggest tasks a man has:

1. To know that he is a man. To know what a man is. You are a man that Abba Father wanted and provided you with the abilities needed.
2. To find your task, which God has prepared for your life. An adventure, a risk, something which is worth fighting for.
3. Conquer your princess. Find the woman whom Abba Father has for you. And love her for the rest of your life.
4. Be a father for your children. And help them to become men and women, fathers and mothers.
5. Lay your blessing upon your descendants
   Lay your blessing upon other people.

And finally my prayer for all of you men:

Abba Father,
The world needs your men, men after your heart.
I have just now blessed them; however you, Father, must confirm my blessing.
So that they will become the fathers who are so desperately needed.
We want to learn from you, Abba Father.
How you love your children and gave the best that you had for them, which was Jesus! For us!

---

[124] Gen 27,33

Abba, let us become more and more like you, so that others will say of us: "Just like his Father!"
Abba Father, please bless all marriages.
And thank you for your overwhelming goodness.

Amen

About Woman

And now to that which we want to share with you about the woman. And what her special relationship to her father is like.

We wrote several things about this in the last chapter.

First of all:
Eve was formed in **Paradise**, in contrast to Adam, who was formed in the wilderness. That means, she was formed in a protected area. That is why Paul says that the man has the function of protecting his wife, which we will see later. And she was formed to be his opposite.

We need to look at the following text very closely:
Genesis 2,18:
„I will make a helpmate suitable for him." is how Luther translated these verses, but the definition found in dictionaries is „helper". Both words are not the exact meaning of the Hebrew words „ezer knegdo", which mean „an opposite help for him". The word „opposite" brings the connotation of someone who is in opposition to the other person. That means that Eve was not a subservient wife who said „Yes" to everything nor an humble hanger-on; instead she was a person with her own rights, who should contradict and rebel, similar to the tradition in the British Parliament, which does not function without „Her Majesty's Loyal Opposition".
One can only be in opposition if the other one takes a position. And that is the task of the man.

The name Eve in Genesis 3,20 has three meanings in Hebrew CHAWWA:
- Giver of Life, or Mother of all that lives. With exception of Adam, all mankind descends from her.
- Speaker. Women often say what men cannot or do not want to say.
- Wise User of Senses. Today we call that female intuition.

According to recent research, all living women of today descend from one woman. Hildegard gave the order for an investigation to be done in the USA, as

Heinrich had done also.

Back to Genesis 2,22:
And God made a woman out of Adam's rib, which he had taken from him, and brought her to Adam.
The Hebrew word for „rib" very seldom means what most German Bible translations write. The translation in the Hebrew Bible means that it comes from the side or the flank. A flank is anatomically necessary, Adam could have gotten along well without one of his ribs.
Rabbis say: Had God commanded the woman to rule over the man, he would have made her out of Adam's head – like Pallas Athena, the patroness of Athens, who was formed from the head of Zeus. Had God wanted her to be Adam's slave, he would have formed her out of his feet, according to the pictoriality of the oriental language. He took her however from Adam's side, because she was to be his equal companion so they could go through life side by side.

Let us take a little time to look at the childhood of a woman. There is a difference in the way boys and girls play. We have never seen any boys who like to play they are drinking coffee. Woman nurture unity and team-work; boys are more interested in competition.

Fathers play a big role in the lives of girls. They are the first male in her life and have a lasting influence upon her. Or not at all, if he is not around. In that case, a big emptiness is there, which is hard to fill later on.

Hildegard's own story.
This is what my parents taught me when I was growing up: Life is nothing but hard work and pleasures are sin. We must respect God, believe the Bible and obey the commands. They were fearful of this punishing God, who can only be appeased through obedience. My step-father was a pious man. Towards the end of his life, he told me the following when we were once alone: „I will be happy to at least have a little place for myself in heaven." He was not able to see himself as a child of God; instead he always felt like he was just an unimportant laborer in God's Kingdom.

I also was convinced that there was nothing to love about myself because I was not able to trust God. And I didn't know why. Many years later after I became chronically ill, I began to work through the problems of my past.

I knew that my father had been in the war when I was born. He had wanted to have a boy; because of this, he showed little interest in me when he visited us. After he left imprisonment at the beginning of 1946 and was at home again, he became sick. And I, a one-year old baby, experienced the slow process of death he went through, since the Americans did not allow any antibiotics to be imported to Germany. When I later wanted to ask my mother about him, she was not able to talk about it. Even all of my relatives refused to talk about my father. Within our family it was Taboo to talk about him because he had been a member of the Storm Troopers and, for this reason, he was shunned by all of my mother's siblings.

Two years after his death, my mother remarried and my loving step-father helped me to have a happy childhood. When I entered the phase of puberty, he unexpectedly changed, which I could not understand, and he was against me and forbade me to do many things. Dancing and celebrations were sin. I was not allowed to finish high school nor to study. For him, girls were less worthy than boys.

Work had to be the most important thing in my life. And I really worked hard in order to earn praise and recognition. But I felt inside that who I was, was not good enough. The feeling that my father did not allow me to enjoy a full, pulsating life nor allow me to be happy, feel free and have a boyfriend, made it all „smell" like sin! This had a negative effect upon my picture of God. I passed along the experiences of my childhood and youth to my relationship to God, whom I wanted to follow, in spite of many negative experiences, because I was afraid I otherwise wouldn't go to heaven.

For these reasons, after Heinrich and I had gotten married, I became active in different Christian organizations, led Bible Study Groups, evangelical meetings and we helped to build up a church, among other things. And then at the age of 40 years of age, I became chronically ill. When the illness was visible, a young lady from our Bible Study Group recommended me to begin a therapy with a doctor, who was an expert in depth-psychology. That was very good for me! I learned to see why I was not able to build up a trusting relationship with God, although I had always tried to and confessed this in counseling. The slow death of my biological father and the rejection of my step-father during puberty, had influenced my outlook upon life and my understanding of God in the following ways for over 40 years:

Girls are not really wanted, unless they can act as boys when around their father. And if the situation is difficult, some fathers leave their wife and children alone. If I work a lot and obey God's commandments, God is pleased with me and will not punish me. But I will never be able to do enough.

That is why I cannot allow myself to enjoy any of the nice things in life. And I became a person whose identity was dependent upon all that I had accomplished.

Only the awareness of my situation in life was not enough to help me get rid of my desire for success, my poisoned lifestyle and my lack of trust, which was the reason why I always condemned myself.

God the Father, however, saw in me an unborn Embryo, traumatized by bombings on Heilbronn in 1944, a deeply injured child after the death of her father and the rejected teenager, who experienced losing her father for the second time.

Due to our move from Frankfurt to Munich in 1996, I again found myself in a situation which was characterized by loss. The two older children stayed in Frankfurt and I lost all of my circle of friends, the leadership of a Christian evangelical organization for women and our Bible Study for young adults. And then, when my husband, because of his job, had to leave me alone during the week, the cup was, so to speak, filled to the brim! After the breaking out of a skin disease, I was befallen with very painful arthritis and had to take strong medication.

I had begun to look at the problems with my fathers and first steps towards healing had taken place, but I was not yet healed into the depth of my soul:

During a Christian conference I asked friends to help me by praying for my healing, that God would heal my soul through the power of the Holy Spirit. I actually felt how I began to be healed. I was filled with great joy and could sing again. And I learned from God my Father that mistakes belong to life. I was able to begin to trust that God was good to me, loved me, just as I was at that moment, even without a halo. That he grants me times of rest and orders me to keep them when I fall back into putting myself under pressure to achieve. And that God the father is joyful over me, over my being a woman, over my interpersonal relationships, over me myself. At the age of 45 I finally began to enjoy my life.

Now back to Psalm 144 which we already have looked at. There is a special message for daughters here:[125]
„...and our daughters will be like pillars carved to adorn a palace."
„...Our daughters will be beautiful as chiseled statues which adorn magnificent palaces."[126]

That is the most important task a father has to fulfill for his daughter. They have been made by Abba Father to decorate palaces. Make them beautiful, be in awe of them, and recognize how lovely they are. They decorate palaces, not huts. Since we as fathers are the first man in the life of our daughters, we must tell them how beautiful they are and how worthy they are to be loved.

Here a quote from Marilyn Monroe, a sex goddess of the last century: "When I was a little girl, no one told me that I was pretty. All little girls should be told they are pretty, even if it isn't true."
It is always true; we just have to learn to look at our daughters through the eyes of our Abba Father. There are great treasures hidden in them!

We like the description in Ezekiel[127] of how God made a woman beautiful, in this case referring to Israel:

6 "Live!"
7 I made you grow like a plant of the field. You grew and developed and entered puberty. Your breasts had formed and your hair had grown, yet you were stark naked.

---

[125] Psalm 144, 12b
[126] Translation from „Die Gute Nachricht", a German Bible translation
[127] Ezekiel 16, 6 14

8 „'Later I passed by, and when I looked at you and saw that you were old enough for love, I spread the corner of my garment over you and covered your naked body. I gave you my solemn oath and entered into a covenant with you, declares the Sovereign Lord, and you became mine.

9 „'I bathed you with water and washed the blood from you and put ointments on you.

10 I clothed you with an embroidered dress and put sandals of fine leather on you. I dressed you in fine linen and covered you with costly garments.

11 I adorned you with jewelry: I put bracelets on your arms and a necklace around your neck,

12 and I put a ring on your nose, earrings on your ears and a beautiful crown on your head.

13 So you were adorned with gold and silver; your clothes were of fine linen and costly fabric and embroidered cloth. Your food was honey, olive oil and the finest flour. You became very beautiful and rose to be a queen.

14 And your fame spread among the nations on account of your beauty, because the splendor I had given you made your beauty perfect, declares the Sovereign Lord.

We are still very impressed by the book of Job, the oldest book of the Old Testament. In the Old and New Testaments daughters and sisters are seldom mentioned. Not the case with Job. He lost all of his ten children through an accident but was given anew the double number of lost animals; but with the children, he was given anew the same number as had died. And they were still his children! Another example to never ending filiation. What is most important to us is the appreciation Job showed for his daughters. All that is written about his sons is how many there were![128]

His daughters were each named:

13 And he was given anew seven sons and three daughters.

14 The first daughter he named Jemimah (Turtledove) , the second Keziah (sweet-scented spice) and the third Keren-Happuch (Cosmetic Compact).

15 Nowhere in all the land were found women as beautiful as Job's daughters;

Many Fathers fail at this point. Because they do not see the talents, the gifts,

---

[128] Job 42, 13-15

the characteristics and beauty Abba Father has put in his daughters: Wonderful names for his children!

Here I, Heinrich, again will step into the gap and make up for what your Father did not do and pray:

Abba Father,
In your name I say to the woman reading this book:
You are like Jobs daughter!
You are wonderfully made, worthy to decorate a palace.
You are loveable, worthy to be loved.
You are a woman after the heart of Abba Father.
And he loves you with all of his heart.
Because you are precious in his sight.
Amen.

After childhood comes the time for education and professional activity. And finally, should one decide, the time of becoming and being a mother.
Today it is expected without a doubt that women carry this double burden.
There is a very interesting passage in the Bible about this:[129]
The passage is usually titled „Praise for the efficient Housewife."
But when we look closer, we discover that it is a description of a working wife, a business women. It has nothing to do with the idea that a women belongs at home, in the kitchen!

10 A wife of noble character who can find? She is worth far more than rubies.
11 Her husband has full confidence in her and lacks nothing of value.
12 She brings him good, not harm, all the days of her life.
13 She selects wool and flax and works with eager hands.
14 She is like the merchant ships, bringing her food from afar.
15 She gets up while it is still night; she provides food for her family and portions for her female servants.
16 She considers a field and buys it; out of her earnings she plants a vineyard.
17 She sets about her work vigorously; her arms are strong for her tasks.

---

[129] Proverbs 31, 10-29

18 She sees that her trading is profitable, and her lamp does not go out at night.
19 In her hand she holds the distaff and grasps the spindle with her fingers.
20 She opens her arms to the poor and extends her hands to the needy.
21 When it snows, she has no fear for her household; for all of them are clothed in scarlet. 22 She makes coverings for her bed; she is clothed in fine linen[130] and purple.
23 Her husband is respected at the city gate, where he takes his seat among the elders of the land.
24 She makes linen garments and sells them, and supplies the merchants with sashes.
25 She is clothed with strength and dignity; she can laugh at the days to come.
26 She speaks with wisdom, and faithful instruction is on her tongue.
27 She watches over the affairs of her household and does not eat the bread of idleness. 28 Her children arise and call her blessed; her husband also, and he praises her: 29 "Many women do noble things, but you surpass them all."

What wonderful recognition of a working wife. What great appreciation!

And now a few remarks about marriage:
We already talked about this when we spoke about the man. Paul wrote the important aspects of marriage in Ephesians, which includes the difficult word about submission.[131]
It begins with:
„Submit to one another out of reverence for Christ!"
This means BOTH to each other! A fine remembrance of the creation of the woman, which we already heard about.
After that there are three verses written for the woman and seven verses written for the man! (If you have not read the instructions to the man in the last chapter, please do that now.) Only three for the woman and double the amount for the man! Summarized from the last chapter, the man gives himself for his wife, protects her and builds her up in all respects.

---

[130] In the German translation the word Byssus is written which is a bundle of filaments secreted by many species of mollusk, that function to attach the mollusk to a solid surface. Byssus cloth is a rare fabric, also known as *seasilk,* that is made using the Byssus if pen shells as the fiber source. (Wikipedia)
[131] Eph 5, 21-31

Now to the text for the woman:
But first, a question: Who would not be willing to entrust themselves to such a man?

Many women, when talking with their friends, talk very contemptuously about their husbands and what all they do not understand. They complain that their husbands are numb to their feelings, that all they think about is sex and sports and that they spend the whole weekend in front of the television. In Ephesians a direct translation from Greek says the following: Wives, let this be your inner attitude: Submit yourselves unto your husbands by your own choice and out of love. For the husband is the savior of the body, as Christ is the head of the church.

Why the savior of the body? Women who had a baby out of wedlock were stoned. If the husband stood up for his wife, as Joseph stood up for Maria and Jesus, he saved her and their baby.

Nonetheless, why should a woman submit herself? Because it helps the husband to grow and mature in his task of caring for his family. They are not as emotionally strong as women, which is seen in their ability to endure sorrow and pain. It can also be seen in the high rate of suicides performed by single men, who are deeply unhappy with their lives.

Men need recognition from women. Wives can help their husbands to become strong by expressing admiration for them. That is what they need the most, that we admire their strength, their skills and their sacrifice for the family.

That is the most important task for married women. Of course she retains her own identity, which we explained when we spoke of „ezer knegdo".

Now to being a mother, in case she wanted to and was able to have children. We don't need to try to explain here what mothers mean to their children. They are irreplaceable. Also because they are to give an important characteristic of Abba Father to their children:[132]

---

[132] Jes. 49,15

"Can a mother forget the baby at her breast and have no compassion on the child she has borne? Though she may forget, I will not forget you!"
And further on:[133]
„As a mother comforts her child, so will I comfort you; and you will be comforted over Jerusalem."
Mercy, pity, understanding. How important this is for children! Especially to experience how God the Father is.

Mothering is so important beyond one's own children, for example, in one's circle of friends, at church and the friends of one's children. Many of them never experienced mercy as a child and, therefore, mothering of children other than one's own, is a wonderful task and experience. God will honor those women, who accept this task.

Finally mothers become grandmothers. There is a wonderful saying: Exactly when a mother is glad her work is done with bringing up children, she becomes a grandmother.

Grandmothers are wonderful! They are there when you need them, they adore their grandchildren, no matter what they do and fill them with sweets when their parents are not around. A lot of positive arguments for grandmothers! But why are there grandmothers at all?
We read a wonderful article in an magazine about them:[134]
„Actually grandmothers should not exist at all: they eat up all the food, which isn't that much for the family anyway, they cannot have any more children (the opposite of grandfathers, at least in principal). Research has shown however that the presence of a grandmother can double the probability of the survival of the grandchildren! The presence of a mother-in-law can increase the probability of her daughter-in-law having a child.
The conclusion of the study is: A grandmother's place is next to her children, being a help which is friendly, never overbearing, never „better than though", just as she'd wished her own mother had been."

---

[133] Isa 66, 13
[134] Nervenheilkunde 2004, Nr. 4, Page 238-240, Schattauer GmbH Stuttgart

And now finally, the grandmother has a very important task.
We can read what Paul had to say about this to his foster son:[135]
„ I am reminded of your sincere faith, which first lived in your grandmother Lois and in your mother Eunice and, I am persuaded, now lives in you also."
Their task is to tell their grandchildren about God the Father, which will lay the ground for trust and faith in him.

That is how it was with me, Heinrich. My grandmother prayed simple children's prayers with my sister and me: Weisst du wieviel Sternlein stehen... (Can you count the number of stars...) or „Müde bin ich geh zur Ruh,...(I am tired and go to rest)...I still have the texts memorized. In this way the grandmother, as well as the grandfather, gives their blessing on to their grandchildren.

And now, we must let you know that Hildegard's roots also began in Africa:

<hr />

[135] 2. Tim. 1,5

However her ancestors changed their route to Europe earlier than Heinrich's did:

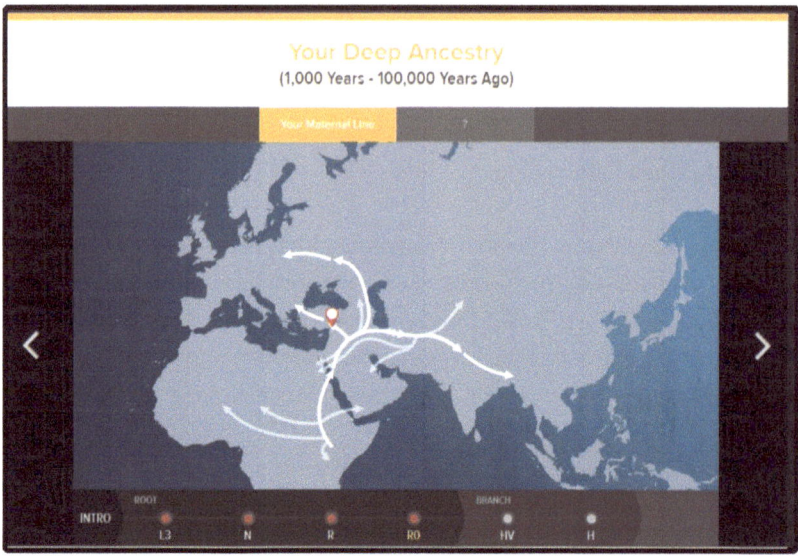

Part 3: ...and his relationship to them.

The Fourth Word.

Now about a word which explains and makes clear the close and intimate relationship between Father, Son and Holy Spirit.
Actually that IS the whole mystery of being a Christian und truly the Good News, as we will hear from Paul!

The fourth Word

What is the fourth most important word after Father, Son and Holy Spirit?
An inconspicuous word in the Bible that is written unbelievably often. Besides that, it is very short, easy to remember. It is the shortest word in the Bible.
If you remember it, you will have understood and possess something very essential.
The word has only 2 letters.

And?

The word is ..... **IN**.

It is amazing how often this word is used in the Bible.

With the meanings **IN** us inside, **IN**to us, always **IN** us. More specifically: God wants to be **IN** us, pour his spirit **IN**to us, live **IN** us, always be **IN** us.

That was his plan from the beginning. **But we didn't want that**.

Let us look at what the Father did to achieve his goal.

Let's begin with looking into the Old Testament:
Genesis 3: God came **IN** the cool of the evening **IN**to the Garden of Eden to talk with Adam and Eve about their day, to listen what happened, to tell them what was on his heart.

It is easy to imagine that on a cool summer evening: when on vacation after a hot day one really enjoys a cool evening. If the day was hot and a breeze cools the air, you can breathe again. And that is a good time to invest in ones relationship by talking together and just enjoying the quietness. God wanted to enjoy that too; he wanted to be with his children. Every day.

You know when it is dark and cold outside in the wintertime, people like to be in a warm room. That provides a good opportunity to talk with each other. And God wants to be with us there also.

However, that wasn't enough for God. He wanted to have someone who would be in his likeness, as is written in Genesis 1,26: Let us make mankind in our image, in our likeness.
A picture, a reflection of us. At eye level: with our Creator!!

But his children didn't want that. We don't want it. At least, not all the time. If we need help, yes, then he should quickly come and help us, in the way we wish.

But God wants to talk with us and let us know what his thoughts are. To be near us, like a father, who holds his child in his arms. However, he got the shock of his

148

life. Let's continue to read:

In Exodus 20, 19ff: The Israelites are happy to be out of slavery (although they longed for the pots full of meat they had eaten in Egypt, but at the same time, knew, if they went back, it would mean they would be imprisoned and slaves again, a situation they had just left. But that was a way of life they were familiar with.)

Their Father wanted to have a relationship with them since he had promised this to Abraham. He told the Jewish people what he, as Father, is like. Und what he had prepared for them.

God gives his 10 commandments, but their messages were immediately twisted and turned around! To be correct, we should call them the 10 forbiddances! Because that is the way they were formulated.

God wanted though to give his people 10 promises. The Hebrew language has no command form, German doesn't either. That is why the commandments are worded as following:

You should do this or not do that.

Actually, however, the wording is in the future tense:

If you love me, you will honor your father and mother.

Whoever honors their father and mother – we are not talking about loving here - will develop healthy self-confidence. You do something good for yourself. That is different from „You must honor your father and mother".

If you love me, - have a close relationship with me, – you will not be able to do anything else than to give my love to others! And that is the original meaning of the 10 commandments.

There God speaks directly to his children in Sinai...but his children don't want to listen. Their fear was keeping them from putting their trust in God. Talk with a holy God, who sends awe-inspiring lightning and thunder? That is down-right dangerous!

They preferred to have Moses as their mediator so they wouldn't have to talk with the living God. It was easier to handle things with Moses. In any case, they at least had someone between them, behind whom they could hide. Had an excuse if they wanted something different. (Moses had not explained well enough which consequences the great number of laws would have over a longer period of time.)

This means: God's first careful attempt to draw nearer to his people failed.

We read in Leviticus that he made another attempt:[136]
"I will walk among you and be your God, and you will be my people."
Before this, we read the promises of Blessings for the Covenant. And after that, three times as many threats of violence, should the Israelites not respect the Covenant. The threats from outside did not help; something within the people had to change.

God kept searching for people **IN** whom his Spirit could live. There are only a **FEW** in the Old Testament. Joshua was one: Numbers 27,18: "So the Lord said to Moses,: Take Joshua son of Nun, a man in whom is the spirit of leadership, and lay your hand on him."

At the end of his life, Joshua, who was leading God's people into the Promised Land, also had to accept that these people were continually worshipping false gods. At the Renewal of the Covenant at Shechem he asks them to make a decision: For or against God (Joshua 24). They vowed to worship only God, but in spite of their vow, fell back into worshipping false gods.

We could look at other situations, for example Gideon, to whom the angel carefully said: The Lord God is with you. Or Simon, **IN** whom God placed unbelievable strength.
As I wrote, only in few specific persons, not in all of his people.

Now a big jump to the Prophets: (We'll leave out David, a man after God's Heart; when he was anointed the Holy Spirit came upon him!)

---

[136] Leviticus 26,12

Here the first suggestion of how „IN" could be used:
Jer. 31, 31-33
31 "The days are coming," declares the Lord, "when I will make a new covenant with the people of Israel and with the people of Judah.
32 It will not be like the covenant I made with their ancestors when I took them by the hand to lead them out of Egypt, because they broke my covenant, though I was a husband to them," declares the Lord.
33 "This is the covenant I will make with the people of Israel after that time," declares the Lord. "I will put my law **IN** their minds and write it on (**IN**) their hearts. I will be their God, and they will be my people."
Or in Zechariah:[137]
 Shout and be glad, Daughter of Zion. For I am coming, and I will live (**IN**) among you, declares the Lord.

Did you know, it doesn't happen from outside but from within, from the heart. God must come **IN**to us. **Wow, but how does that happen?**

God made a new Plan:[138]
Verse 24ff: For I will take you out of the nations; I will sprinkle clean water on you. I will give you a new heart and put a new spirit **IN** you.
V 27 And I will put my Spirit **IN** you and move you to follow my decrees and be careful to keep my laws.

For the first time God proclaims here that he will put his Spirit **IN** us. And that happened at Pentecost. He doesn't want to try to speak with us anymore through laws, agreements, miracles, covenants or other ways, instead he wants to be **IN** us.

But, how is that supposed to happen? He, who made heaven and earth, live **IN** us? **How should HE have enough space there?**

In order for us not to have a reason again to say that God has no idea how difficult life is on earth, he puts his ingenious plan into action, which he'd made

_____

[137] Zecha 2,10
[138] Ezekiel 36

151

before people were created.

HE shows us himself how that should work.

HE comes **IN** the person of Jesus.

The God who created everything wants to show us what he looks like, living **IN** a person. He does himself what he is planning to do with us.

I will not handle here the fact that Jesus had a further task, namely, to take our guilt upon himself.

When Jesus was 12 years old he told this to his parents, who had searched for him for days after a celebration in the temple: Why were you searching for me? Didn't you know I had to be **IN** my Father's house?

What were Jesus' **first** words when he, at the age of 30 years, preached in public? Mark 1,15: The time has come and the kingdom of God has come near. Repent and believe the good news!

IN Jesus the Kingdom of heaven came closer to us than ever before. God **IN** one person. Now it is possible to experience what that means. How God planned this! He took a great risk to come closer to us. Nearer than ever before.

Luke 17,21

The Pharisees ask him how it would be when the Kingdom of God comes. Jesus answered: „...the kingdom of God **is** in your midst." The Kingdom of God has come **IN** Jesus, but not **IN** the Pharisees! Religion hinders the **IN**! The eyes of Religion are on laws, ordinances and rituals. Nothing is invested in relationships, instead in Knowledge. Compare Genesis 3,5: „For God knows that when you eat from it your eyes will be opened, and you will be like God, knowing good and evil." (Luther 2017) I will know, but not told by God the Father or the Holy Spirit, what is good and bad for me.

And what do we do?

John 6, 30: „ So they asked him, "What sign then will you give that we may see it and believe you? What will you do?"

We want to see miracles, that our prayers are answered.

That Jesus does something for us.

We want God to give us something, but we don't want him.

We want to go into the world for Jesus, but we don't want to **BE** Jesus there.

We want to stay ourselves and Jesus should help us with our work.

How God is doing, doesn't interest us.
We don't even think about being interested in God, what moves him, what makes him happy, what he plans. (Not what we think he might be planning.)

What does Jesus do instead? He gathers disciples around himself to show them what life is with him and from him.
With mediocre success.
They are interested in sitting at his left or right side and ask who is the greatest among them.
Yes, he is interested in making more out of his disciples but not as they think it should be done:
John 4,14:
„but whoever drinks the water I give them will never thirst. Indeed, the water I give them will become **IN** them a spring of water welling up to eternal life." We ourselves should be the wellspring of life, for others of course. It is logical that a wellspring is not thirsty, isn't it?

And that is why something **IN** us needs to change.

The first thing that Jesus gives us here is his first commandment.
And what does it say?
No, not: „Love the Lord your God with all your heart and with all your soul and with all your strength and with all your mind'; and, 'Love your neighbor as yourself.'
In Matthew 24,36 one of the Pharisees asked what the **greatest commandment in the law** is and Jesus' answer was the recitation of two verses from the Old Testament, namely Deuteronomy 6, 4+5.

Jesus gives a new commandment, his commandment:
Twice in the Gospel of John:
John 13,34 and John 15,12. In my wife's Bible the following is written on one side of a opened double page:
That is MY commandment: that you love one another, as I HAVE loved you.
Love = present, have loved = past = EXPERIENCE.

Can Jesus command us to love? NO

We have to have experienced love first, before we can love others.

But that cannot happen through obeying commands or decrees, living according to rules etc., it needs something stunningly new. Jesus talks about that in John 17, in his High Priest Farewell Prayer, at the end of his mission on earth:

What does he pray? What would we have prayed, had we been in his situation???
He did not pray for good leaders and lively churches, evangelizations, no missions projects or other commandments, great miracles and healings, supernatural ways of life, no, no, no, something completely unexpected:

V 12a: While I was **IN** their presence, I protected them and kept them safe by that name you gave me.
V 13: I am coming to you now, but I say these things while I am **still** in the world, so that they may have the full measure of my joy with**in** them.

Jesus first concern is that we have his joy with**in** us. Which joy? His Joy! Not something that we are happy about but the joy of Jesus, which is **IN** us and will spill over to others. Think about the wellspring of water we just talked about. That came also from within.

And now the climax:
V 20
My prayer is not for them alone (he means his disciples who were with him) but I pray also for those who will believe in me through their message.
We are definitely meant here.

Another comment: In the following verses Jesus spoke directly to his Father. Here he always uses the word „Abba", a childlike address; yes, even a childlike address filled with trust. This word does not exist in the Greek language; for that reason the word Father is used here. We must read this text as a familiar request, for that reason I used „Abba".
And now definitely for us:

V 21

that all of them may be one, Father, just as you are **IN** me and I am **IN** you. May they also be **IN** us so that the world may believe that you have sent me.

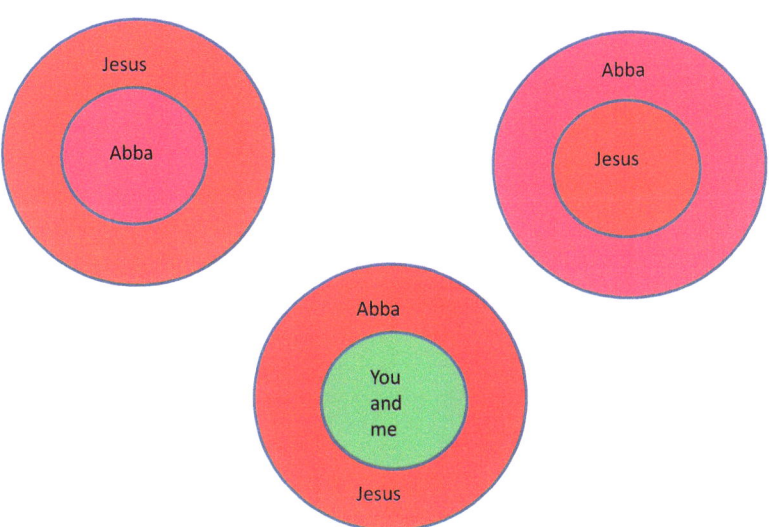

Stefan Dries expressed this wonderfully: To be in the Father, in the Heart of God. No matter to which side I turn, I always hear God's heart beating: Bum Bum, I love you. Up and down: Bum, Bum. I love you. Front and back it sounds: Bum bum, I love you. Right and left I hear only: Bum Bum, I love you. Were we to lie with our ear on Jesus' breast, as John did, **one** ear only would hear: Bum Bum, I love you. The other however would be turned to the world and hear other whisperings.[139]

V 22
I have given them the glory that you gave me, that they may be one as we are one.
V 23
I **IN** them and you **IN** me—so that they may be brought to complete unity. Then the world will know that you sent me and have loved them even as you have

---

[139] Quote after Stefan Dries, CZ Karlsruhe 2014

loved me.

John 17, Verse 23

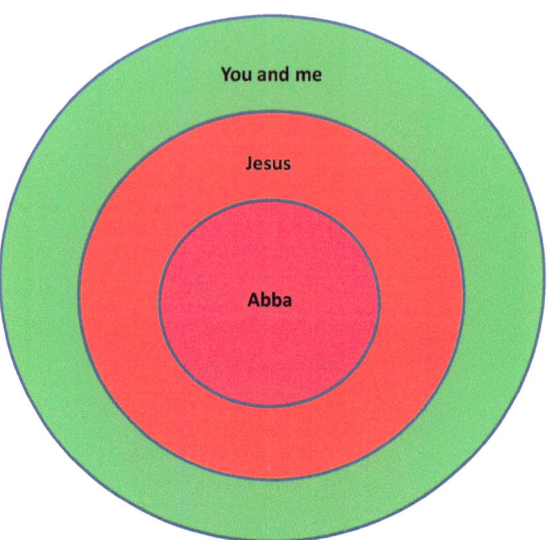

Dear friends, how that can all happen at the same time (it **is** like that though), is more than I can fathom! It is very clear and explicit that Jesus and the Father want to have intimate fellowship with us. They are not so far away from us that we have to call them, no they are **always** **IN** us. Not just now today, no: They are always there. The best description we have found is: living in one another.

All week, every day, Day and Night. Always. For all of Eternity.

Paul described this in Galatians like this:[140]
19 My dear children, for whom I am again in the pains of childbirth until Christ is formed **IN** you...“ Paul chose the Greek word Morpho, which means inner shape; we use the word Morphology, which means the inner structure. In contrast, the outer structure is described as scheme, or pattern. Paul wants Jesus to be **IN** us to change us and the fruits of his presence should spread from inside to the outside (how we live or behave).
In Romans[141] we read: „Greet Andronicus and Junia, my fellow Jews who have

---

[140] Gal 4,19

been in prison with me. They are outstanding among the apostles, and they were **IN** Christ before I was. (Translation of Lutherbible)

Matthew gives us another reason[142]

15 Peter said, "Explain the parable to us."

16 "Are you still so dull?" Jesus asked them.

17 "Don't you see that whatever enters the mouth goes into the stomach and then out of the body?

But the things that come out of a person's mouth come from the heart, and these defile them.

19 For out of the heart come evil thoughts—murder, adultery, sexual immorality, theft, false testimony, slander.

20 These are what defile a person; but eating with unwashed hands does not defile them."

When the Father, Jesus, and the Holy Spirit are **IN** us, the good thoughts of God will come out of our hearts. Paul emphasizes this in Romans:[143]

„...And hope does not put us to shame, because God's love has been poured out **IN**to our hearts through the Holy Spirit, who has been given to us." (NIV)

It doesn't mean that it will be poured out, it has already been poured out!

Knowing

We want to show, using a context which is not real easy to understand, how close and intimate this relationship is seen by God, our Father.

The Hebrew word for this is **ido**.

Adam knew Eve: 4,1:

And Adam knew Eve his wife and she conceived und bare Cain, and said: I have

---

[141] Romans 16,7. Very important here, that the name is Junia and not Junias like some later transcribes wrote. They could not imagine, that a woman had become an apostle! The name Junias does not exist in Roman language, but Junia.

[142] Matt 15,15ff

[143] Romans 5,5

157

gotten a man from the LORD. In Hebrew:[144]

u	e adam	ido		ath-chue	ashth u
and	the human	he-knew (->)		Eva	woman of him

u		ther	u	thld		ath-qin
and		she-is-becoming-pregnant	and	she-is-giving-birth (->) Cain		
u		thamr				
and		she-is-saying				

qnithi	aish	ath	ieue
I acquired	man	with	Yahweh

In German this passage is often translated with the word „to know".
The true meaning though is:
„Adam slept with...", to be exact – he „knew" Eve, his wife, as in the verses 17
and 25. The Hebrew word means „to know / get to know" **IN** personal
encounters.

We find the same word ido in Exodus 33,12 and 17, where the relationship
from God to Moses is spoken about.
„I know you by name and you have found favor with me."

... u	athe	amrth	**idothi**	k	b
	shm				
and	you	you-said I-know you		in	name

Please do not misunderstand this, but God the Father, Jesus and the Holy Spirit
want to have such a close relationship with us.

And now we come to the highlight of the whole story. To be specific, we find out
how we can experience this.

In ....

---

[144] Taken from: Interlinear Scripture Analyzer ISA Basic Version 2.1.4 von 2010

...the Communion.

Jesus announced this – in his harsh speech:

John 6,53
Jesus said to them, "Very truly I tell you, unless you eat the flesh of the Son of Man and drink his blood, you have no life in you.

Who will have the abundant fulfilled life? Those **IN** whom he is.

This speech made many of his followers turn away from him. But he saw this was **the** chance to show us how he can and wants to be **IN** us. To be able to experience him, not only imagine it.

And finally at the Last Supper he said to his disciples:

Mark 14,22:
„While they were eating, Jesus took bread, and when he had given thanks, he broke it and gave it to his disciples, saying, "Take it; this is my body." He must be **IN** our bodies.

And in the next two verses:
„Then he took a cup, and when he had given thanks, he gave it to them, and they all drank from it. "This is my blood of the covenant, which is poured out for many," he said to them. His blood must go **IN**to us. We belong to those many.

That is what Abba and Jesus and the Holy Spirit want: to be **IN** us. To bring out our originality. To be the fountain of Living Water **IN** us and make us to be that also. Rivers of Living Water should flow out of us.

God wants to have a very close relationship with us, almost closer than we can imagine. The best comparison is that of a pregnancy, during which the child is in the mother, who provides it with all that it needs. And also gives it protection. Perhaps you now want to say: „That sounds nice and good, but I don't notice or feel it".

Then we have to read Revelations 3, Verse 20:

„Here I am! I stand at the door and knock. If anyone hears my voice and opens the door, I will come in and eat with that person, and they with me."

How does this happen?

A process begins.

Let me explain this to you using the example of my Life-House, my Life as a House.

Jesus is standing outside and knocks, I open the door (to my heart).

That is a very strong door with only a handle inside to open it. There is no way to open the door from outside.

„Oh my goodness! Who is out there ? There's no way I can open up now!"

Perhaps I will invite him in the next time he comes.

In the tidy

Living Room = My chocolate side. And he will say: I like it here. However, he is interested in more than just the living room. Maybe when he visits again he can go in the

Kitchen = my job or in the workshop (for men) or look at my work. Then later the **Bedroom = my dreams and fears before I go to sleep.** And, especially for men, my **sexuality.** Here he will say: I know all about it and it is all good. When he comes again

the **Bathroom = and there I am standing naked** in front of him. Naked! And he will say: I like you. In my presence you will not feel naked. Because you are fully accepted. Being ashamed is not necessary because you are my child." The first time young children feel naked is when they separate from their mother. In that case, feeling naked would be a sign of separation, the close relationship, which was there before, is gone. (As with Adam and Eve!) That is important for children so they can develop into independent adults; It's the opposite with the children of Abba Father! Be a child with your Father, not an adult who leaves his Father.

 Perhaps I can even show him **the attic, my plans for the future** and what I would like. He says:"let us dream together." After that maybe he can go in the **cellar where things are which are not so pleasant,** which I have stowed away or had to locked up, or I would not have survived. Experiences which have to be walled in.

He says: „ I will heal you and release you from your burden of bad memories. I know what happened and I suffer with you."

Ask him to come in. Abba will not come in without an invitation. He is a Gentleman! And he will not be shocked at what he finds. He knows everything anyway!

How can **I personally** know that God is **IN** me?
When I pray I especially am given many ideas and thoughts, which I would otherwise never have thought about.
For example, Heinrich's project for schools and kindergartens in Africa. I NEVER had the wish to go to Africa. But now I must do it, because God changed something in me.[145]

Was does it mean when Papa, Jesus and the Holy Spirit are **IN** us?
Probably most of you have a cell phone. We can always be reached, can talk with everyone all the time or at least write a text message. We have the security that we can always rely on it. If we lose the cell phone or the battery is empty, we have a problem.

We can compare this with when our Father, Jesus and the Holy Spirit are **IN** us, but what is even better is:
We can never lose them, their batteries will never get empty, we can always talk to them,
they protect us, they will never leave us and are always with us. And the sim card is our identity. That's how the Father planned it.

Paul speaks of this as **THE** big mystery of being a Christian:[146]
26 the mystery that has been kept hidden for ages and generations, but is now disclosed to the Lord's people.
27 To them God has chosen to make known among the Gentiles the glorious riches of this mystery, which is Christ in you, the hope of glory."

---

[145] More Information about our work in Africa under www.l-a-p.eu
[146] Col. 1, 26-27

No one before us, not Abraham, not Moses, not David, none of the great leaders of Faith, ever experienced this: Jesus IN us, God the Father IN us, the Holy Spirit IN us.

Some say: I do not feel God **IN** me!
It is similar to the stomach: When it growls, we know that is needs something or is hungry.
Or it's similar to our heart: when it „knocks", we are emotionally touched.
Or when you have over exerted yourself, you know it also.
But otherwise? Our stomach is there and is doing his job, the heart just the same. The Father, Jesus and the Holy Spirit are **IN** you, working and fulfilling you more and more, like sour dough, which finally spreads out into all the dough, making it all sour.

Prayer:
Father, Papa, Abba. You want to be **IN** me. Together with Jesus and the Holy Spirit.
And I should be **IN** you:
So: I cannot understand that yet.
But I want to! I will be at your disposal.
We will be at your disposal.
I invite you to live **IN** me.
I will prepare a place for you **IN** my heart.
So you can change me to be the person for whom you gave your life.

And because you are **IN** me, I'll hear it.
Open the ears of my heart, so they can hear.
And the eyes of my heart, so I can see it.
And because I am **IN** you, I am protected as in my mother's womb.

Abba, Jesus and Holy Spirit, please come **In**to me anew.
I need you all **IN** me.
So that I experience who I am **IN** your eyes:
Abba's beloved child!
Amen.

That has further consequences: John worte:[147]

„No one who lives **IN** him keeps on sinning." At first this verse is hard to understand, is aggravating. Who of us doesn't sin anymore! But the verse means: when we are **IN** Jesus, **IN** the Father, we cannot, at the same time, be separated from him -= to sin!

The Verse continues:

„No one who continues to sin (=who has separated himself from Jesus and the Father) has either seen him or known him."

Those who have really tasted what it means to be **IN** the Father, don't want to leave him anymore!

---

[147] 1. John 3, 6a

About Responsibility

Now a very important subject in our relationship to Abba Father: **Responsibility.**
All Pastors love to preach about it, parents and teachers talk about it quite often.
Everyone talks about responsibility, politicians want it, we all have it or think we
have it, but what does the Bible have to say about it?

So, let's get out the concordance. I found this word only two times in a
concordance of the New Testament written by Luther, translation in 1984:
1.Peter 3,15:
„...But in your hearts revere Christ as Lord. Always be prepared to give an
answer to everyone who asks you to give the reason for the hope that you have.
But do this with gentleness and respect."
and
Jeremiah 40,10: „I myself will stay at Mizpah to represent you before the
Babylonians."

In the Elberfelder translation, in Acts 22,1 we find this:
„ "Brothers and fathers, listen now to my defense."

The word „Responsibility" is not found in the English Standard nor in the King
James Versions of the Bible!

In all cases it has to do with accountability. That is the one meaning of
responsibility and it is biblical. At the Convent in Jerusalem, Peter gave account
about his mission to the Heathens. You probably all know about the story of
Captain Cornelius.[148]

However, responsibility in today's language usage includes these four aspects:
1. To accept and take over a job, with which I identify and invest myself .
2. To ensure carrying out of the job by controlling, surveying and coaching.
3. To have the competence and the strength to carry through with the job.
4. To give account of what was accomplished. In jurisdiction the question

---

[148] Acts 10

of guilt caused by insufficient completion is **always** combined with being responsible.

When we carry out our responsibility, we have laid a burden, a load, or more explicitly, a responsibility upon the other person. Best of all, without influencing the other person.

Certainly all of us who have worked have experienced the following: You were made responsible for a job which went wrong. In most cases, never for something that was a success. Your boss gets all of the credit. And usually they did not have the competence – not to mention being able to do the right thing – to influence and organize things.

In the „Gute Nachricht“ (Good News) Translation: There are nine examples of using the word responsibility in the New Testament. If we look at Luther's additional Bible verses, it is always a job that is fulfilled.
Matthew 24,47:
Luther: „Truly I tell you, he will put him in charge of all his possessions.“
GN: I assure you: The Lord will give him the responsibility over all of his possessions.

This means there is a shifting of the meaning in the new translations. What originally was called a task is today called a responsibility.

That is why responsibility is a burden, a load for us today, which we cannot really carry.
Even if our boss gives us freedom to decide as we see best, we have no control over all factors which influence our job: the weather, the world economy, an illness and many other things are not in our hand.

The Pastor has been given the responsibility that the church will function. Woe to him if it doesn't! Then everyone will pounce upon him!
Is he really capable? Does he have it all? Is he completely over burdened? (A sure sign: the many burnouts among pastors!)

Let's not continue to talk about pastors.

What responsibility do I carry?

Which have I allowed others to lay upon me?

Or more tragic: Which have I laid upon myself?

Perhaps during childhood?

Which is about to make me collapse?

The responsibility for the unity of my family.

For my sick parents, for my siblings, family and in the church.

Perhaps for my mother as the substitute for the father who didn't exist anymore or was never there or was sick or unable to cope with life or was divorced. Or, just the opposite by taking over the responsibility for the father. That can burden us even until this day.

Usually things like that happened when we were children and helped us to survive. But what are the consequences?

Today responsibility means to do everything, watch out for everyone and everything, plan, take consideration for others and carry the consequences for everything so that power is mine.

Can the pastor or church leader really take over the responsibility for the church?

In Ephesians 5, 23 is written: Christ is the head of the church.

Who carries the responsibility?

The one who is head of the church or the one who serves the church and is accountable for what they do?

Of course it is he, the head of the church: Jesus.

He wanted the church. He built it up. He developed it. He takes care of it.

Jesus gave us tasks to do, but did not lay the burden of being responsible for them upon us. He carries that himself.

We could never carry that. How would it be possible? Then we would really have to have everything under control.

Let us look at some of the tasks Jesus gave others to do:

The Sending of the 12 Disciples in Matthew 10, 5ff: in German the New Geneva Translation.

5 These twelve Jesus **sent** out with the following instructions: "Do not go among

167

the Gentiles or enter any town of the Samaritans.

6 Go rather to the lost sheep of Israel.

7 As you go, proclaim this message: 'The kingdom of heaven has come near.'

8 Heal the sick, raise the dead, cleanse those who have leprosy, drive out demons. Freely you have received; freely give.

9 "Do not get any gold or silver or copper to take with you in your belts

10 no bag for the journey or extra shirt or sandals or a staff, for the worker is worth his keep.

His warnings and instructions continue, almost until the end of the chapter. So many instructions of what the disciples should do. BUT no threats: „Woe unto you if it doesn't work out. If you are not successful, I will be mad!"
No words like: „ I lay the responsibility of this project being successful upon you!"

Another example: The Sending of the 72 disciples in Luke 10, 3ff.

3 Go! I am **sending** you out like lambs among wolves.

4 Do not take a purse or bag or sandals; and do not greet anyone on the road.

5 "When you enter a house, first say, 'Peace to this house.'

6 If someone who promotes peace is there, your peace will rest on them; if not, it will return to you.

By the way, this doesn't mean to always go „without any armor"! We have to see what the task entails.

Luke 22,35ff:

35 Then Jesus asked them, "When I sent you without purse, bag or sandals, did you lack anything?" "Nothing," they answered.

36 He said to them, "But now if you have a purse, take it, and also a bag; and if you don't have a sword, sell your cloak and buy one.

The Feeding of 5000 in John 6,5ff

5 When Jesus looked up and saw a great crowd coming toward him, he said to Philip, "Where shall we buy bread for these people to eat?"

6 He asked this only to test him, for he already had in mind what he was going to do.

7 Philip answered him, "It would take more than half a year's wages to buy enough bread for each one to have a bite!"

8 Another of his disciples, Andrew, Simon Peter's brother, spoke up,

9 "Here is a boy with five small barley loaves and two small fish, but how far will they go among so many?"

10 Jesus said, "Have the people sit down." There was plenty of grass in that place, and they sat down (about five thousand men were there).

11 Jesus then took the loaves, gave thanks, and distributed to those who were seated as much as they wanted. He did the same with the fish.

12 When they had all had enough to eat, he said to his disciples, "Gather the pieces that are left over. Let nothing be wasted."

13 So they gathered them and filled twelve baskets with the pieces of the five barley loaves left over by those who had eaten.

Phillip did not want to accept this task because it seemed impossible to complete. We will be held accountable for such situations. What is possible or impossible is decided by the employer: It is impossible for me, but, with God, it is possible.

The responsibility for impossible tasks is held by Jesus and his Father.

I love the feeding of the 5000 for a second reason:
Because of the little boy.
He could have said: That is my lunch, how is that supposed to be enough for everyone? It is better that I keep it.
Why do you think that you can have it?
And the little boy would have hindered Jesus' miracle taking place. For me he is the hero of the story, of course, after Jesus.

Even Jesus handled according to the wish of someone else! And here he makes an account of what he did.
John 17,4ff
3 Now this is eternal life: that they know you, the only true God, and Jesus Christ, **whom you have sent.**
4 I have brought you glory on earth **by finishing the work you gave me to do.**
5 And now, Father, glorify me in your presence with the glory I had with you

169

before the world began.

6 "**I have revealed you to those whom you gave me out of the world. They were yours; you gave them to me** and they have obeyed your word.

7 Now they know that **everything you have given me comes from you.**

8 For I gave them the words you gave me and they accepted them. They knew with certainty that I came from you, and they believed that you **sent** me.

And now to one of the most important tasks:

The Great Commission in Matthew 28,18ff

18 Then Jesus came to them and said, "All authority in heaven and on earth has been given to me.

19 Therefore go and make disciples of all nations, baptizing them in the name of the Father and of the Son and of the Holy Spirit,

20 and teaching them to obey everything I have commanded you. And surely I am with you always, to the very end of the age."

Did Jesus say anything here about us having responsibility? Nothing!
In these verses we can learn how responsibility is laid out in the Bible!

Verse 18: Mir, Jesus, the mandator, has been given all authority. That corresponds with the 3rd aspect in the explanation of responsibility (see above). Jesus carries that responsibility.

Did you read the following: „Watch out like a shitty dog so everyone lives as I commanded"? No!

Verse 20: Jesus said himself: I am with you always. I am the coach and have everything under control. That is the 2nd aspect of responsibility: You have a task; I am the Mandator.

Of course we will be held accountable for how and what we did, following the leading of the Holy Spirit. But the Mandator has the power and the control.

This is what is left for us to remember:
Aspect 1: Accept the task, invest ourselves in it. Of course here is meant the task which the Father gave to us, not what we or someone else laid upon us.
Aspect 4: Give an account of what we did.

170

Our Father gives us the strength we need. In 2. Corinthians 3, 4 and 5 we read:
4 Such confidence we have through Christ before God.
5 Not that we are competent in ourselves to claim anything for ourselves, but our competence comes from God.

We can find many other commissions in the Bible.:
Entrusted money: Don't bury it![149]
The Parable of the workers in the Vineyard[150] : Who is held responsible? The owner of the vineyard, the winemaker.

And one more thing: The family in Ephesians 5:
The passage about submission, which turns many women stomachs when they read or hear about it. Let us read very carefully:
Submit unto one another!

The man is given a long list of assignments and tasks, how to treat his wife as well as his children. The word "head" is used here to describe the function of protecting his wife and his children. The head of the family is Jesus.

We are to serve, we have a job. The responsibility is carried by Jesus, the Holy Spirit and the Father.

Paul wrote the following to Timothy: 1. Timothy 6,14:
"Keep this command without spot or blame until the appearing of our Lord Jesus Christ."
The job, not the responsibility. But we can hear the call to accountability "behind the lines".
Here is more very explicit advice from Paul in 1. Corinthians:[151]
5 What, after all, is Apollo? And who is Paul? Only servants, through whom you came to believe—as the Lord has assigned to each his task.

---

[149] Luke 19,13ff
[150] Matt 20,1 - 16
[151] 1. Cor 3, 5-9

6 I planted the seed, Apollo watered it, but God has been making it grow.

7 So neither the one who plants nor the one who waters is anything, but only God, who makes things grow.

8 The one who plants and the one who waters have one purpose, and they will each be rewarded according to their own labor.

9 For we are co-workers in God's service; you are God's field, God's building.

What the Lord gave him to do, not for which things the Lord makes him responsible. Upon whom does it depend? On the Father, for whose work we unite our strength.

Yes, but what if the mission fails?

A first example is Jona:[152]

1 The word of the Lord came to Jonah son of Amittai:

2 "Go to the great city of Nineveh and preach against it, because its wickedness has come up before me."

He didn't want to go and left quicker than you can imagine. Because of the seemingly impossibility to evangelize to a city the size of Nineveh, with 120,000 inhabitants. But God lovingly brought him back with the help of the whale. Then Jonah left after making the comment: „God, you'll see that it won't work out." Surprisingly and unexpectedly for him, his mission was a success. No, not surprisingly, it caused him displeasure! But that is another story.

Paul in Athens:[153]

He is determined to convince the Athenians to believe in Jesus. That was not possible. Instead he grounded a church in Corinth, which later became a lively growing church.

Joseph in Genesis 37ff:

God revealed his task to him in a dream. Then at a later time his father, Jacob, asked him to go and see how his brothers were doing and he left to carry out his

---

[152] Jonah 1, 1-2

[153] Acts 17 and 18,1

father's request.

You know the story: He is sold to slave traders, later sold again to an Egyptian citizen Potiphar, whose attendant he became, but whose wife had him put into prison. Then his career advancement in Pharaoh's court and the rescue of his family clan by moving them to Egypt. The interesting thing is: His career advancement took place in one day, from being a prisoner to becoming Pharaoh's attendant, the most important person in the government after Pharaoh!

That is the best example of this saying:

God can make something good out of our mistakes, or the mistakes of others! He is the only one who can do that!

Joseph said in Genesis 50, 20:

„You intended to harm me, but God intended it for good to accomplish what is now being done, the saving of many lives."

Peter, who denied Jesus:[154]

Peter denies Jesus three times in a rather uncritical situation, when a servant girl approaches him because of his dialect.

In spite of this, Jesus gives him the commission at feed his lambs and care for his sheep[155], after Peter's repentance to Jesus. Interestingly, Jesus asks Peter three times if he loves him, which is the same number of times that he denied Jesus. Another comment here: In the Greek text Jesus asked him twice: Do you love me with the Agape-love, with the love with which the Father loves us. Peter answered both times with the Philei-love = the love for a friend. The third time Jesus asks him using only the Philei-love.

And Jesus ends this conversation with the command: Follow me!

Peter became an important man in the early church and in the conversion of heathens.

Finally my, Heinrich, story:

I was not always such a diligent pupil in school, not to mention during puberty. I didn't always do my homework. Had to repeat the 11th grade, which deeply hurt me. I cried out to God, but that didn't help. I just was not on the same

---

[154] Luke 22,24ff
[155] John, 21,15-17

wavelength with both of my language teachers, who both gave me the grade F (I had failed to pass that school year).

After that I changed schools.

A fellow pupil introduced me to my future wife; we will soon celebrate our 50th wedding anniversary.

In my High School diploma I was given, instead of 2 Fs in my languages, a C in French and a B in English. And today I can speak both languages rather fluently! And what is even more wonderful – I have given several lectures and sermons in English!

As you can see, God our Father can make out of everything just what he planned it to be.

If we could only leave the responsibility in his hands. Even from the beginning of time, Adam and Eve had problems with this. They wanted to decide themselves what is good and what is bad.

And that went completely wrong. It has even gotten so far today that what is bad is simply explained away. And even up until today, the world does not know how to decide what is good or bad without the help of the Holy Spirit, nor knows what good and bad really mean.

Let us leave the responsibility to him, who wants to take it over. And above all, has the capability. Because he carries the whole world, which is also our lives.

Why did Jesus say in Matthew 18:

„And he said: "Truly I tell you, unless you change and become like little children, you will never enter the kingdom of heaven."

Which responsibility belongs to children?

NONE. Not even in criminal law!

The younger they are, the more dependent they are on their parents and accordingly trust them more. So much in this area has been destroyed in us. The more responsibility we take upon ourselves, the harder it is to give it into the hands of our Father.

We can read in Jeremiah 7,23[156] that Jesus has taken over the responsibility for our lives:

„ I will be your God and you will be my people.“

God has also taken over the responsibility for the human side of us, for the second part of this verse is not an invitation, but an explanation to Israel.

We could interpret this passage as follows: I will be your God and make sure that you will know who I am and live in fellowship with me.

God the Father has only children. And he wanted each one.

He wants to take over the responsibility for us and our lives.

For he knows that we would be overwhelmed because we do not have the capability for that.

That is why he waits with open arms for us to come to him.

I want to pray for you as a reader:

Father, you wanted us and took over the responsibility for our lives. Thank you for the tasks you give to us.

Thank you, Father, that I don't have to be God.

Lord Jesus, many people are carrying responsibilities which were laid upon them and are too much for them. And we have taken responsibility upon ourselves because we couldn't bear a situation anymore. You said: „Come to me, all you who are weary and burdened, and I will give you rest. Take my yoke upon you, for my yoke is easy and my burden is light.“

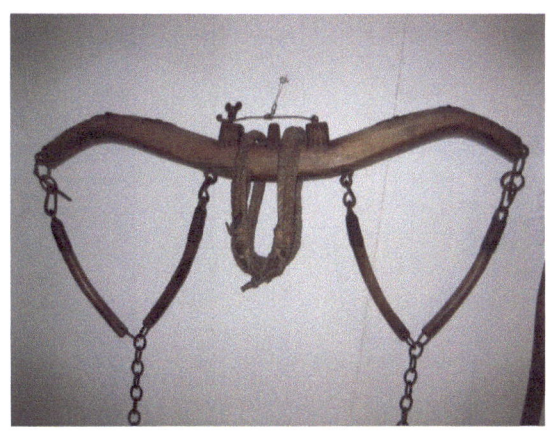

Yoke means that Jesus walks next to us to show us how to carry out our tasks.

---

[156] Jer 7,23

Holy Spirit, I ask you to please help me and us to let go of the false responsibilities we have laid upon ourselves. If we are not able to shake it off, please send us someone who can help us.

And if someone wants to lay new responsibility upon us, then we can say: „Jesus' yoke is on my shoulders, I don't have room for anything else."

Thank you.

Amen.

The Lord's Prayer.

Now we want to look at the Lord's Prayer as the most important prayer in the Bible.

A Rabbi taught his pupils how to pray, just as John the Baptist did. (His followers still exist in Syria!) Jesus' disciples asked him how they should pray. Jesus gave them „The Lord's Prayer" as a sample prayer. Let us look at it to see what it says about the relationship to Abba God. It is quoted in the New Testament in the two Gospels Luke and Matthew.

The version in Luke:[157]
Father,
hallowed be your name.
Thy Kingdom come.
Give us this day, our daily bread.
And forgive us our trespasses, as we forgive those who trespass against us.
And lead us not into temptation.

The version in Matthew:[158]
Our Father in heaven, hallowed be your name,
your kingdom come, your will be done, on earth as it is in heaven.
Give us today our daily bread. And forgive us our debts, as we also have forgiven our debtors.
And lead us not into temptation, but deliver us from the evil one.

A wonderful, simple prayer in which, in spite of its length, everything is said that is important about our relationship to Abba God.

The version found in Matthew has become the version which is prayed by all Christians. However in the first sentence it includes the extra words „in heaven". The transposition of Abba God into a distant heaven has become accepted. The

---

[157] Luke 11, 2-4
[158] Matt. 6, 9-13

Father is far away in heaven, not near to us, as Jesus said:[159] „The kingdom of heaven has come near." God the Father is enthroned in heaven, the same as Zeus in Greek mythology.

But in spite of this, the first sentence is revolutionary! Never before did any human call God „Father". The Jews did not even trust themselves to speak out God's name Yahweh because it was so holy. As a result of this, they crucified Jesus. Actually we read here only Abba = Father. The name „Abba" has the status of a foreign Aramaic word in the Greek text. It expresses unflinching faith in the nearness to God, but doesn't express intimate confidence. „Father" is addressing God with respect. God is not put down on a level of triviality nor of a buddy. Perhaps Matthew wanted to underline this by using the extra words.

The further structure of the prayer is similar to that of the 10 Commandments: God comes first, then we. The first part is theocentric, with God the Father in the center. That switches around the middle of the prayer: On earth, as it is in heaven.
In the second part of the prayer the ones addressed are „us" or „we".
The first part is: Asking that God be God. Not that we first of all want to have something, but the Father should be and remain God.
The second part: Asking that the life of believers may be a success: our daily needs, living with respect and love together with our fellowman, ethical uprightness and eternal salvation.

In this prayer one can feel the trembling in the presence of the holy God, but a basic trust and fascination are stronger. Our Father, my Father. A trustworthy frame for prayer, familial and personal. This form of prayer differs from heathen babbling, which Jesus warned to avoid.[160]
The Lord's Prayer expresses a personal relationship to God.
In the following we will look more closely at the Lord's Prayer, using the translation from Prof. Knut Backhaus.

Salutation:

---

[159] Matt 4,17
[160] Matt 6,7

Our Father who art in heaven

Today we would begin such a prayer with „Dear God". A salutation which expresses a certain degree of trust in God, but doesn't expect God to be very near. The Bible never speaks of a nice God. God is not nice! Today nice means either availability (be a nice child) or it expresses weakness. Jesus shows us a loving God. And even more important: as we have already described in former chapters, God the Father, who made heaven and earth, desires to be near his children.

We are not talking about a „God". That could mean one of many different Gods. And everyone would have another understanding of what is meant.

It begins with „Our Father in heaven". „Our" emphasizes the fellowship Jesus has with his Father's children. An unbelievable allowance for us, for all people. We are allowed to speak with Jesus' Father as he does.

This prayer reflects the intimate relationship between God and his Son Jesus. Jesus is not copying any ancient Jewish prayers and he doesn't speak the formal Ab (=Father), but the Aramaic Abba. Actually a Lulling word of little children, as we have already mentioned. However the content is not a Lulling word, is not at all infantile, but, is instead the greeting for Papa by his grown sons. That is best understood in the Russian language. It is a respectful greeting, meaning „dear little Father".

So that it doesn't sound too banal, Matthew adds „in Heaven". Here respect resonates without fear or distance to the Father. Christians may call God their Father, because Jesus taught us to pray that way in the only prayer he handed down to us. Quite a venture! Actually something unheard of! That is not possible in any religion in the world. Even according to Jewish understanding, the Father's task is not so much to offer comfort in and through the laws, but to educate his children.

Jesus speaks of „Our Father", not your father. He immediately brings us into fellowship with his Father. With these two words he makes us to his brothers and sisters, without any preparations or requirements. His Abba-Theology in two words![161]

1. Petition

Hallowed be Thy Name. Eugen Bieser[162], a great Catholic theologian, whom both of us heard in lectures, said: „Which name is to be hallowed? **Father** is his name!"
John said the same thing:[163]

11 I will remain in the world no longer, but they are still in the world, and I am coming to you. Holy **Father,** protect them by the power of your **name**, the name you gave me, so that they may be one as we are one.
12 While I was with them, I protected them and kept them safe by that name you gave me.

This request should remind us of the greatness of the partner with whom we are speaking, before we begin thinking about ourselves. In conversations we should concentrate on the one opposite us before we begin speaking about ourselves and our requests. The word „hallowed" is kept imperative. It expresses God praising himself, passivus divinus. That means, God should hallow his Name. We ask that God is God! That God is Father. Just as his name. Through our names we have power over things. Rumpelstiltskin, from the German fairy tale of the same name, was ruined when people found out what his name was. The evil spirit is done with when he has to tell his name.[164]
God alone has power over his name. And he wants to be named Father. The request is written in Aorist of the Greek language. This Grammatik form, a verb, describes a punctual event which remains active in the future. God the Father should enforce his holiness in individual situations. Before it is revealed at the end of time.
Our praise of his name will not increase his glory, but he blesses us through that.

2. Petition

---

[161] Matt 12,50
[162] Eugen Bieser, emeritus Professor at the LMU Munich, the first appointed holder of the Romano Guardini Chair
[163] John 17, 11-12
[164] Mark 5,9

The Kingdom of God come.

In a Prayer of Praise, according to Jewish understanding, one has to talk about the Kingdom of God. This Coming is theocentric; humans do not build God's Kingdom on earth.

The time has come! Jesus spoke this statement, which is recorded at the beginning of the Gospel of Mark: [165] „"The time has come," he said. "The kingdom of God has come near. Repent and believe the good news!"

The Kingdom of God comes through Jesus' Proclamation, shown through his actions.

Fighting for the Kingdom of God is not biblical. God himself will bring about his Kingdom.

3. Petition

Thy Will be done – on earth, as it is in heaven.

Here we can again say human action cannot bring about God's Kingdom; what the Father decides, will be done. It does not stand in competition with human will. That happens when we act morally. Surprisingly this level does not exist for Jesus.

However it has nothing to do with me making myself smaller so that God can be greater. Of course people should act morally. Here the Father is asked to hold the world together.

God's Will is always to heal. That is why moral does not help us here. The motive is not to make people smaller but that God's wish of Salvation for all men can be realized.

To be more definite: I should wish the same or help that God's Will take place. Isn't God almighty? Can he not do everything? Yes, of course, however, his will can only be done if I agree. Know what his will is. Not only in me. What is now reality in Heaven, should come step by step upon earth, from one place to another, at the dawn of the Kingdom of God. We are not the ones who should bring heaven on earth, because it would probably become Hell on earth! Instead we should concentrate on knowing what God's Will is, as Jesus told us.[166]

---

[165] Mark 1,15
[166] John 5,19

It is possible to understand the first three requests this way: God our Father needs us. As we said above, he wants to express himself through us, and through our prayers too.

Your Will be done on earth, as in heaven. God is really a strange God. Isn't he almighty?

From his point of view, yes. For his love is omnipotent and we can consent to it. His will can only be carried out if we agree; His Will can only be carried out if His Will becomes ours also. And that is what these requests are about.

Changing our perspective:

4. A petition and, at the same time, the focus of the prayer.

Give us this day, our daily bread.

The most important thing we can pray for our own sakes. Jesus suggests for us to live in the present and not in the past nor in the future. Don't worry about the upcoming day.[167]

Most people want something which they don't have yet or something they lost, instead of living for today.

The most important word in the petition: daily requirement.

The Greek word here is EPIOUSIOS: According to Origines, this word doesn't exist in the Greek language. Someone made it up!

(Made up of the words epi= over, ousia = Substance; epi +ousia = over the substance)

In the original text an Aramaic word is written which has no Greek equivalent. Other translations also don't offer satisfying results: Vulgata: excessive bread. Itala: daily. Syrian: continual bread. Pheschita: our necessary bread. Coptic: for tomorrow. Maebo: the coming bread.

An in script on a wall in Pompeii reads: Daily food.

This perhaps reminds us of the Eucharist, Christ himself, God's Word as spiritual bread. A link to bread for communion and through that, to Jesus. That was unheard of in Palestine and is surely not the original meaning.

The meaning has more to do with what was necessary to keep alive. What I need to live this day so that my soul is not hindered in its constant seeking of

---

[167] Matt 6,34 Therefore do not worry about tomorrow, for tomorrow will worry about itself!

God.

Jesus, as the "wandering Charasmatic",[168] lived from one day to the next; for this reason the meaning "daily ration of bread" seems to be the most plausible explanation.

Bread for life for the present day. A clear reference to the feeding of manna to the Israelites, as written in Exodus 16. For the same purpose: The people in the desert were fed the same way as the wandering charismatic.

Let us look at the daily provisions from Abba in the present. He provides daily for us.

Another interpretation is: Providing for the day to come (Ethiopia). That is the best interpretation, although not the highest level, to be found in their language. God provides for you today so that you have no needs tomorrow. It is enough to think until the end of this day.

We can look at "bread" from a wider perspective: Our day and time suffers not from a lack of bread but from the meaning of daily life. In this case it would mean: One day is enough time to find the meaning of life.

Now back to the little children we mentioned in the previous chapters: A little child does not think about tomorrow.

Looking at this topic through the eyes of a child, we can see ourselves as day-labourers, who live from God's hands to our mouth, so to speak.

And as Eckhard Nordhofen[169] said: The heavenly bread as our daily supply for food and meaning of life.

5. Petition:

And forgive us our debts, as we also have forgiven our debtors.

After the body is fed and satisfied, we find out how to handle guilt in the best way. Guilt is a financial metaphor about giving and taking. First the OTHER person has to have been forgiven before we turn to our Father with this request. Why?

The space in which we live with one another could be poisoned, relationships

---

[168] A quote by Prof Backhaus, Lecture "Jesus of Nazareth" WS 2015/16 at the LMU Munich und Lecture "The culture of Prayer in the New Testament" WS 2014/15 LMU Munich

[169] Eckhard Nordhofen: Brot und Zeit und Philologie (Bread, Time and Philology), Frankfurter Allgemeine Zeitung vom 27. 5. 2015

could be impossibly or very heavily burdened. Brain and Attachment Research as well as Psychology were completely unknown for people of that time. Or results of Forgiveness Research.

Prof. Dr. Konrad Stauss explains forgiveness in his book[170] outstandingly. Unforgiving has serious effects, independent of the Christian faith. Human relationships are poisoned. If the problems are repressed, the whole person can become poisoned, not only his relationships. Just as a virulent ryegrass and rotten apples can poison a field.

The process of forgiving, as practiced by Matthew and Jesus, is not done just through speaking conciliatory words, but is very hard work! Forgiveness as a task of not allowing the earth to be continually contaminated. Coming to terms with guilt is not carried out so often today, although that has to do with the success of human existence.

Here we look at the parable of the unforgiving servant[171]. Forgiveness, which we receive, we should give to others.

Conflicts are not the problem, there was enough of them in the first church and between Paul and Peter. But through forgiveness we can get out of the vicious circle of guilt.

6. Petition

Lead us not into temptation.

This petition is hard to understand.

God leads us into temptation? The devil does that, for example, when he tempted Jesus.

First of all, God leads to temptation: Psalm 11,5; 26,2; Exodus 20,20 in the sense of testing us.

At the time of early Christianity, problems with this came about:[172] „When tempted, no one should say, "God is tempting me." For God cannot be tempted by evil, nor does he tempt anyone; but each person is tempted when they are dragged away by their own evil desire and enticed."

---

[170] Prof. Dr. Konrad Stauss, Die heilende Kraft der Vergebung, (The Healing Power of Forgiveness) Kösel Verlag München, 2. Auflage 2012

[171] Matt 18,23 ff

[172] James 1, 13-14

Or interpret it this way: And lead us not into doubting. This interpretation though has no philological basis. There are 60 different interpretations of this Greek term, but doubting is not one of them.

„Lead us INTO Temptation." Jesus did not say that!

In the Qumran writings[173] we find the following: Do not bring me into situations which are too difficult for me.

Latin translations explain this so:
Do not allow us to be led into temptation. Do not let us be tempted.
Lead us in such a way that we do not fall into temptation. Lead us out of temptation.

Luther's interpretation: You keep our bodies from tempting us.
Eugen Bieser interpreted: Lead us out of temptation.

But prayers are not logical, they are passionate. Temptation is a theme.
One last explanation: Since this has to do with a prayer during the Last Days, the temptation of this era = falling away from God. Our Father should lead us in such a way that we do not give up our faith.

Now a reference to Jesus, how he handled temptation:
In Luke we read:[174]   First of all Jesus was baptized and filled with the Holy Spirit. Then the Spirit led him into the desert. There he was tempted by Satan. And he did not fall into temptation because of his disarming answers from the Bible.

7. Petition
but deliver us from evil.
Jesus sees all the dangers in the life and faith of those who pray, coming from that which is bad. Or is evil. Both can be a temptation. The Kingdom of God stands firmly against evil.

---

[173] Qumran 11, 24
[174] Luke 3, 21 to 4,1

Presbyter, Calvinists and the East churches see evil as masculine, the Catholic and Lutheran churches as neutral. Although Luther does refer to it in the masculine.

In our world today evil does not exist anymore. It has been „pathologised".[175] That means someone is not evil, they are just sick. With that argument it is not possible to find salvation, because the Ill have to be medically treated .

We think, the neutral opinion is the central one. God should forgive us and, at the same time, eliminate evil at the root.

A good addition here is Jesus' High Priestly Prayer as written in John 17. It says: „My prayer is not that you take them out of the world but that you protect them from the evil one." Taking them out of the world would be an easy solution, but that is not what Jesus wants. He wants us in be in the world.

Why does the Lord's Prayer end so open?
It ends where it began, it isn't completely finished, but continues in our life!

Soon the Doxology was added (for thine is the Kingdom and the Power and the Glory forever and ever.) because an end to the Prayer was needed. Perhaps someone had a bad conscience in making only requests and not praising God.

Theologically this prayer is the sum of all of what is Christian. The center of the Sermon on the Mount, which Jesus preached, as Moses did. Even Tertullian[176] looked at this prayer as the sum of all what is Christian.

Thomas of Aquin[177] wrote: The Lord's prayer is not only the most perfect prayer, but also the order of the list of petitions within the prayer are of great importance.
As Bertold Brecht said[178]: „First comes the bread, then morality."

---

[175] Quote from Prof. Armin Nassehi, Lecture Introduction in Sociology, WS 2013/2014 LMZ Munich

[176] Tertullian (150 to 220 n. Chr.) was an early Christian writer. His real name was *Quintus Septimius Florens*.

[177] Italian Dominiker, Philosopher and Theologian (1225-1274)

[178] German playwright and lyricist (1898 - 1956)

About Eternal Life

We have written a lot about Abba Father's relationship to his children. Since we will spend eternity with him, here are some thoughts about eternal life.

To do that, we have to understand how time is embedded in eternity. Eternity was before and is after; between that is a period of time in which the world was created, which still exists, and will someday be replaced by a new world:[179]

„1 Then I saw "a new heaven and a new earth," for the first heaven and the first earth had passed away, and there was no longer any sea."

In the following sketch we have tried to make clear how this is meant. Eternity is not represented by the arrowed timeline, but is a timeless term, perhaps comparable to the blank area showed in the sketch.

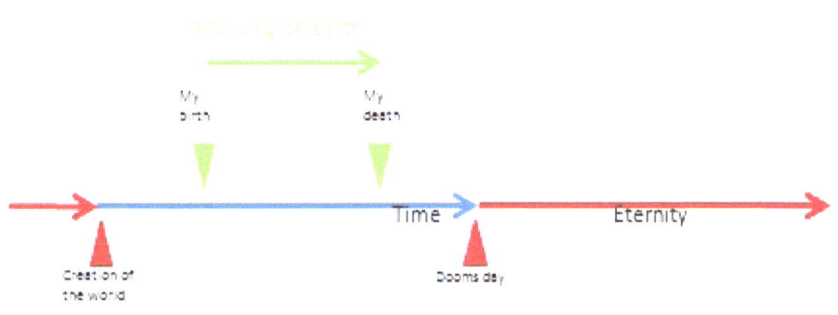

Let's take a closer look at the short blue timeline and draw along it our lifetime.

---

[179] Rev 21,1

But first a comment about the scientific theory of the Big Bang. The theory states that time did not exist before the Big Bang suddenly took place. If that is how it happened, then our Father triggered this emergence, possibly at the beginning of the blue timeline. Our Father existed before the Big Bang, for who could have otherwise triggered it? No physics scientist claims that something can evolve out of nothing.

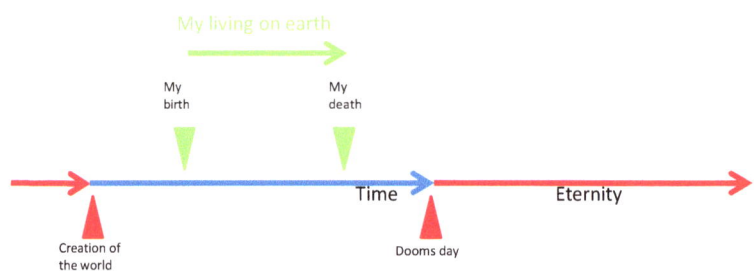

When will my eternal life begin with my Father?

We can find a first answer in the Gospel of John:[180] „Now this is eternal life: that they know you, the only true God, and Jesus Christ, whom you have sent." We find a comment about the word „know" in the chapter „The Fourth Word" under ido.
It begins when we decide to follow Jesus and continues from that point in time. It is not only a decision for Jesus, but for the Father also! This sentence is written in the verb tense Aorist of the Greek language!
So that means that eternal life begins here on earth, goes through a transition when we die and continues in the presence of our Father.

---

[180] John 17,3

John wrote in his first letter:[181] „As for you, see that what you have heard from the beginning remains in you. If it does, you also will remain in the Son and in the Father. And this is what he promised us—eternal life."

Paul writes in Ephesians:[182] „And God raised us up with Christ and seated us with him in the heavenly realms in Christ Jesus."

John explains this again:[183] „And this is the testimony: God has given us eternal life, and this life is in his Son. Whoever has the Son has life; whoever does not have the Son of God does not have life." With this knowledge our sketch looks like the following:

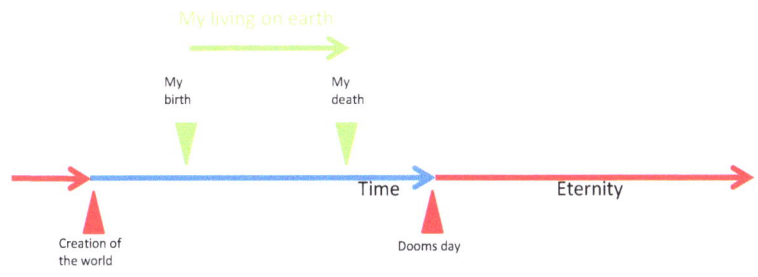

Remark: The time between my death and my resurrection cannot be shown, as it is not known. Due to my decision to follow Jesus, is my Father's election for me, planned before the word was created, effective and my eternal life begins with my Father.

This life with our Father has three periods, as we can see in the following chart:

---

[181] 1. John 2, 24-25
[182] Ephesians 2, 6ff
[183] 1. John 5,11-12

189

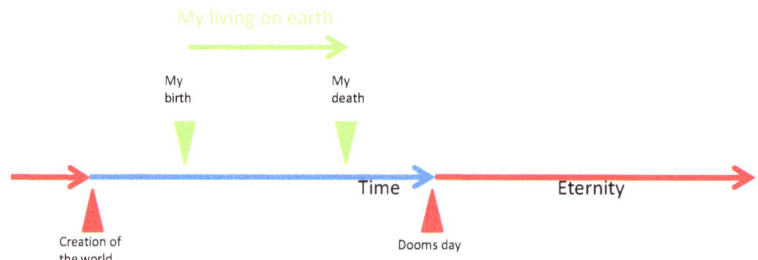

One period before my death, one period before my resurrection and one „period" in Eternity.

The first period has a great influence upon the third period. Especially upon the tasks we have to do during that time. The idea that we will sing „Hallelujah" all day, as is the case in the humorous Bavarian story of an angel, who'd lived in Munich before he died (Muenchner im Himmel)",[184] is not found in the New Testament!

About the resurrection we can read in John 11:[185]
„Jesus said to her, "Your brother will rise again." Martha answered, "I know he

---

[184] "Der Münchner im Himmel" is a story from Bavaria. Alois, a porter, dies and goes to Heaven. Sadly to say, he does not like it there, eating Manna and singing Hallelujah all day long. So God orders him to tell the Bavarian government what his advice is. But on the way there, Alois makes a visit to the Hofbräuhaus, a beer-drinking hall, drinks a mug of beer, and another one...and that is why the Bavarian government is still waiting today for God's advice

[185] John 11, 23-25

will rise again in the resurrection at the last day." Jesus said to her, "I am the resurrection and the life. The one who believes in me will live, even though they die."

We emphasize with full assurance that our salvation is never to be questioned, it was a work of grace, nothing we can earn and (see Adoption) will never be revised.
Now to John:[186] „My sheep listen to my voice; I know them, and they follow me. I give them eternal life, and they shall never perish; no one will snatch them out of my hand."

However, how we live our lives here on earth has relevance upon eternity. This remark should not make us afraid or increase our fear, but instead, show us just the opposite – which opportunities we have been given to increase our talents (see God the Father and I).

Let us begin with Luke 19, 11-26
11 While they were listening to this, he went on to tell them a parable, because he was near Jerusalem and the people thought that the kingdom of God was going to appear at once.
12 He said: "A man of noble birth went to a distant country to have himself appointed king and then to return.
13 So he called ten of his servants and gave them ten minas. 'Put this money to work,' he said, 'until I come back.'
14 "But his subjects hated him and sent a delegation after him to say, 'We don't want this man to be our king.'
15 "He was made king, however, and returned home. Then he sent for the servants to whom he had given the money, in order to find out what they had gained with it.
16 "The first one came and said, 'Sir, your mina has earned ten more.'
17 " 'Well done, my good servant!' his master replied. 'Because you have been trustworthy in a very small matter, take charge of ten cities.'
18 "The second came and said, 'Sir, your mina has earned five more.'
19 "His master answered, 'You take charge of five cities.'

---

[186] John 10, 27-28

20 "Then another servant came and said, 'Sir, here is your mina; I have kept it laid away in a piece of cloth.

21 I was afraid of you, because you are a hard man. You take out what you did not put in and reap what you did not sow.'

22 "His master replied, 'I will judge you by your own words, you wicked servant! You knew, did you, that I am a hard man, taking out what I did not put in, and reaping what I did not sow?

23 Why then didn't you put my money on deposit, so that when I came back, I could have collected it with interest?'

24 "Then he said to those standing by, 'Take his mina away from him and give it to the one who has ten minas.'

25 " 'Sir,' they said, 'he already has ten!'

26 "He replied, 'I tell you that to everyone who has, more will be given, but as for the one who has nothing, even what they have will be taken away.

First a few comments about the setting of this parable:
Jesus was probably referring to a historical happening: Herod's son, Archelaus, who followed his father to Judea, had to travel to Rome to obtain acknowledgement from the Emperor to be his Father's successor. As a matter of fact, the Jews had sent a delegation to follow him, hoping to hinder his mission. However the Emperor granted Archelaus the King's royalty.

Figuratively speaking, Jesus represents the man from the royal family. He descends from King David. The people expected him to take over the government within a short time. However he tells about a trip to a foreign country to obtain a King's Royalty. He will return to his father and come back to the people as a King. In the meantime, he instructed his servants how to use the talents given to them. Worked with them! Luther translated: Use them! Others translated: Use them to bring profit.

As we have seen before, our Father gave us gifts, even more than we can imagine! And he expects us to use them in the best way possible for us. That applies to our lifetime on earth. For when Jesus comes again, time will come to an end.

After the return of the King, accountability is given. The King wanted to know what had been done with the talents. The first servant increased his talent by ten times the original value. He was given ten cities to rule over. And was highly praised. Just as the second servant, who increased his gift by five times the value. And he was given five cities to rule over.

We can see that being faithful with small gifts, which, referring to this parable, was only one pound, but one city would have brought thousands of times more than the one pound, has great influence on the King's Kingdom. The third servant's gift (interestingly we are not told what happened to all the servants), which out of fear he hid, was taken away from him.

Similar to the story of the prodigal son, in which the younger son inherits the robes of his father, as well as his ring, fattened calf, etc.

So, let us keep this in mind: the King expects us to develop our gifts.

Let us look at what Paul has to say about this subject in 1.Corinthians[187]:

10By the grace God has given me, I laid a foundation as a wise builder, and someone else is building on it. But each one should build with care.

11 For no one can lay any foundation other than the one already laid, which is Jesus Christ.

12 If anyone builds on this foundation using gold, silver, costly stones, wood, hay or straw,

13 their work will be shown for what it is, because the Day will bring it to light. It will be revealed with fire, and the fire will test the quality of each person's work.

14 If what has been built survives, the builder will receive a reward.

15 If it is burned up, the builder will suffer loss but yet will be saved—even though only as one escaping through the flames.

Paul knows that through God's Grace he has been given the talent to lay a foundation. That is without a doubt the most difficult job when building. If the foundation is not correctly built, construction cannot succeed.

And then others come along and continue building with other materials. Invest the talents they have been given. Everyone in this example are construction workers, who do not always use the appropriate materials, either because of ignorance or to save money.

---

[187] 1. Cor 3, 10-15

The day of accountability will come here also. In this example, the fire which will prove the quality of the building. It is true that all the construction workers are rescued, but many have lost everything, standing there with empty hands, just like the servant, who buried his pound in his handkerchief.

Summarized, what we do with our talents here on earth will influence what happens to us in eternity. Johannes Hartl[188] expressed it in this way: "Here on earth we have a mandate which influences our mandate in Eternity. This is a Training Camp, the real job begins in Eternity."

Additional verses on this subject are found in Hebrews:[189] "For here we do not have an enduring city, but we are looking for the city that is to come." The city mentioned here is the same one as found in Luke.

One last thing: The Day of Judgment.
We explain this very simplified, in Revelation and other verses other aspects are described.

In Ecclesiates[190] we read the last verse in this book: „For God will bring every deed into judgment, including every hidden thing, whether it is good or evil."

In John 5 [191] we read:
„Moreover, the Father judges no one, but has entrusted all judgment to the Son, "Very truly I tell you, whoever hears my word and believes him who sent me has eternal life and will not be judged but has crossed over from death to life."
Jesus will be the judge.

In court, besides the judge, there are those who are guilty, that is us, that is me. And there will be a prosecutor, who is Satan:[192] „For the accuser of our brothers and sisters, who accuses them before our God day and night, has been hurled

---

[188] Dr. Johannes Hartl leads the Prayer House in Augsburg
[189] Hebrews 13,14
[190] Proverbs 12,14
[191] John 5, 22 and 24
[192] Rev 12,10. See also 1.Tim 3,6b; Job 1 and 2

194

down." This passage actually describes the end of the court hearing.

There is also an advocate, who is the Holy Spirit:[193] „ And I (Jesus) will ask the Father, and he will give you another advocate to help you and be with you **forever.**"

Then the accusation will be presented. Jesus the Judge will look in his book and say: „This accusation has already been settled. Mr. Prosecutor, I can tell you on which date that took place." Which date? On the day when Jesus forgave us all of our shortcomings.
„Do you have any more accusations? All the pages in my book about this person are unwritten, all existing entries are marked as deleted!"[194] The prosecution is dismissed."
Paul wrote about this in Colossians:[195]
„But now he has reconciled you by Christ's physical body through death to present you holy in his sight, without blemish and free from accusation."

Paul describes it in Romans[196] in this way: „Therefore, there is now no condemnation for those who are in Christ Jesus."

After that Jesus will, as did the King in the verses in Luke, request accountability and define our new tasks.
What we have achieved in the world does not count. We found a wonderful explanation of this:

„And on that day, which is not a day anymore – he will perhaps say:
Why do you step up before me with your little baskets full of achievements, which are as little as empty hazelnuts?
Did I not free you from this?
I want to know this: Did you excite others about life, as I did in you?"

---

[193] 1. John 2,1
[194] This can best be described with the example of a Land registry to a plot. All debts from the past are marked as deleted, but can still be read! That applies also to right-of-way etc.
[195] Col 1,22
[196] Romans 8,1

That is what he gave us our talents for.

We already have the Big Payoff:
We are righteous!
That means we are righteous in the Father's Judgment.
Jesus won this for us.
That is our assurance.

Because Abba loves us.

Epilogue.

Thanks to Abba.

We have tried to emphasize the perspectives of our Father which are important to us, which we have experienced and which, at least in our opinion, are all too seldom seen and talked about.

It is important for us not to talk about moral, but rather about what is written in God's word. Morals are dependent on society and changeable. As you like. Independent from God and his plans.

Summarized, three sensations about our Father:

—   The accommodating Father.

—   The God three-in-one **IN** us and we **IN** him.

—   our final Adoption through our Father.

There is one passage in the Bible which summarizes the whole contents of our book:[197]

1"For we know that if the earthly tent we live in is destroyed, we have a building from God, an eternal house in heaven, not built by human hands.
2 Meanwhile we groan, longing to be clothed instead with our heavenly dwelling,
3 because when we are clothed, we will not be found naked.
4 For while we are in this tent, we groan and are burdened, because we do not wish to be unclothed but to be clothed instead with our heavenly dwelling, so that what is mortal may be swallowed up by life.
5 Now the one who has fashioned us for this very purpose is God, who has given us the Spirit as a deposit, guaranteeing what is to come.
6 Therefore we are always confident and know that as long as we are at home in

---

[197] 2. Cor 5, 1-10

the body, we are away from the Lord.

7 For we live by faith, not by sight.

8 We are confident, I say, and would prefer to be away from the body and at home with the Lord.

9 So we make it our goal to please him, whether we are at home in the body or away from it.

10 For we must all appear before the judgment seat of Christ, so that each of us may receive what is due us for the things done while in the body, whether good or bad."

Perhaps some questions have not been answered yet. That is all right. For our Father has not reached the end of our journey with him. By the way, people who were Christian, but not yet named Christians, were called by the name Hodos. This word, Hodos, means those who are on the way. The best example is the Disciples from Emmaus in Luke[198].

And we are not theologians, who have the exact answer for everything.

Now just one more question:

Is it possible to learn fatherhood (and motherhood) ?

Is that possible, after all we have written as explanations and descriptions of who God is?

Yes, we can experience this through doing the following every day: Let's just imagine we are sitting on the Father's lap, day for day, enjoying looking at Him. It is very worthwhile taking time for this! Then his Spirit can begin to speak to us and our Father will begin to show us his love for us.

And we can ask him the questions which we have carried in our hearts for so long! Just like a little child.

But what do I do, if I don't feel the Father?

All we need to do is pray: „Father, I come to you to sit on your lap because I want so very much to feel your presence and to talk with you."

To take advantage of my inheritance, my rights, even if it feels quite unfamiliar. The more time we spend so close to him, the more love Abba can fill us with,

---

[198] Luke 24, 13-33

even to overflowing. We need to have experienced this. Jesus said „Love one another, as I have loved you."[199] The present for the others, the past for me. It is absolutely necessary that I have experienced the Father's love, or else one day I will become very desolate and frustrated.

Our heartfelt thanks to you, dear reader, for not having laid this book aside. We pray that Abba will reveal his love to each of us.

Now, at the end, we express our thanks to the following persons, who were vital in the conception and development of this book:
Susan Schuelke, who dedicated a lot of her heart to translate our book into English. And the tremendous work she put in.
Angela and Wolfgang Bienert for the corrections and incredible, time-consuming editing work.
Prof. Dr. Siegfried Scherer and Dr. Sigrid Scherer for the spiritual inspiration.
Most of all, Bernhard Otto for this topic, which he spoke about in the Father Seminars held by the Marburger Kreis, at which we had the honor to take part in.
And to our teachers at the Ludwig-Maximillian-University in Munich, Germany:
Prof. Dr. Knut Backhaus, Prof. em. Dr. Eugene Bieser and Prof. Dr. Armin Nassehi.

And to our Abba, who always loves us.

Hildegard and Heinrich Becker

Summer 2017

---

[199] John 13,34

Appendix:

"My baby loves me just the way that I am."
We have replaced „baby" with „Abba"; Daddy would also be a good choice.

Don't need no copy of Vogue magazine
Don't need to dress like no beauty queen
High heels or sneakers he don't give a damn
My Abba (baby) loves me just the way that I am
My Abba (baby) loves me just the way that I am

He never tells me I'm not good enough
Just give me unconditional love
He loves me tender and he loves me mad
He loves me silly and he loves me sad

He thinks I'm pretty, he thinks I'm smart
He likes my nerve and he loves my heart
He's always sayin' he's my biggest fan
My Abba (baby) loves me just the way that I am
My Abba (baby) loves me just the way that I am

When there's dark clouds in my eyes
He just sits back and lets 'em roll on by
I come in like a lion and go out like a lamb
My Abba (baby) loves me just the way that I am
My Abba (baby) loves me just the way that I am

He thinks I'm pretty, he thinks I'm smart
He likes my nerve and he loves my heart
He's always sayin' he's my biggest fan
My Abba (baby) loves me just the way that I am

He thinks I'm pretty, he thinks I'm smart
He likes my nerve and he loves my heart

Don't see no reason to change my plan
My Abba (baby) loves me just the way that I am
My Abba (baby) loves me just the way that I am

A comment about the translation:
nerve = Courage.

Biographical Data

Heinrich Becker

Undergraduate Studies in Mathematics and Business Administration at the Technical University in Berlin.

Until 2009 leading position in major companies in the Department of Logistics.

Speaker at numerous national and international Conferences for Logistics.

Co-author of „Handbuch Kommissionierung", Heinrich Vogel Publishing Company, Munich 2009

Co-worker in a counseling-oriented Christian network since 1970.

Speaker and preacher in numerous churches in Germany and abroad.

1. Chairman Learn-Apply-Proceed e.V. (www.l-a-p.eu)

Hildegard Becker

Training as a teacher afterwards 11 years of teaching.

Mid 1980s takeover of the management of Breakfast Meetings for Women in Frankfurt.

After the work-related relocation of her husband, take-over of the Management of Breakfast Meetings for Women in Munich.

Co-worker in a counseling-oriented Christian network since 1970.

Speaker at Breakfast Meetings for Women in German-speaking areas.

Author of „Die Lebensmitte kommt bestimmt" (Mid-Life will surely come), Johannis Publishing company, Lahr 1999.

Sermons in numerous churches in Germany and abroad.

Other books by the authors:
About Hearing

The purpose of this book is to give each reader courage to depend completely upon the Holy Spirit when praying with and blessing others and when practicing counseling. Through Listening. He knows exactly what each individual person needs and what can help them the most. 25 years of experiencing the working of the Holy Spirit have been woven into these accounts.

Building upon Listening Prayer and Listening Blessing, we are led into Listening Counseling. This is not a book to teach a method, so that we can learn how to counsel as if following a recipe, but shares the accounts of the miracles which we experienced as we were closely led by the Holy Spirit. How well he knows his children, how he lovingly brings to their attention what is hidden and can be a help to us. So that the Father's children can finally enter and live in freedom.

BoD – Books on Demand 2013
Norderstedt, Germany
ISBN978-3-7322-4713-4

notice: